Loving TEACHERS

WISDOM, BEAUTY, AND BLESSINGS

Loving TEACHERS

WISDOM, BEAUTY, AND BLESSINGS

DR. GERRY NOLAN

LEONINE PUBLISHERS
PHOENIX, ARIZONA

Published by Leonine Publishers LLC
Phoenix, Arizona
USA

ISBN-13: 978-1-942190-25-7

Library of Congress Control Number: 2016941818

Printed in the United States of America
10 9 8 7 6 5 4 3 2 1

Visit us online at www.leoninepublishers.com
For more information: info@leoninepublishers.com

for

Dave and Marie

Contents

Foreword ix

A Note to the Reader xi

Personal Prologue:
The Tale of Two Teachers 1

Part I

Personal Connection 13

Chapter One:
Know Our Students Well 19

Chapter Two:
Vision 39

Chapter Three:
Acts of Kindness 57

Part II

Professional Connection 93

Chapter Four:
Give Our Best 97

Chapter Five:
Expect the Best 111

Chapter Six:
Meet Students Where They Are 127

PART III

CHARISMATIC CONNECTION 145

Chapter Seven:
Enthusiasm 151

Chapter Eight:
Empathy. 167

Chapter Nine:
Respect 189

Chapter Ten:
The Big Finish 207

Personal Epilogue:
The Long and Winding Road 225

Bibliography. 231

About the Author 239

Foreword

Reflect with me, back to a time when you as an educator entered a new job setting. Ponder the emotions surrounding that situation. These emotions are most likely somewhat similar, whether as a first-year teacher or someone with significant experience. As I reflect back on my first face-to-face meeting with Gerry Nolan, that was exactly the situation I was in.

My heart beat wildly as I waited in my office for Mr. Nolan, the new superintendent, to come and introduce himself to the elementary principal hired only a few months before him. We knew nothing about each other. A warm smile and handshake greeted me as he sat in the chair across from my desk. His first words to me after our initial greeting were, "Tell me about your family." My heart rate quickly returned to normal and I was immediately at ease. That moment was the beginning of a lifelong connection between Gerry Nolan and Gayle Holte.

Gerry Nolan, in a single word, is about "connections" with those he encounters, and in the case of this book, the students we serve. He believes in his heart, and supports the belief with evidence, that our students will learn only when they feel valued and cared for by the adults in their educational environment. The many personal accounts of students themselves found on these pages only serve to confirm the importance of loving educators in their lives. There is new meaning for the word "love" as it relates to the education profession.

The author lives his philosophy in everyday encounters with students, staff, parents, board members and others in the educational environment. He inspires those around him to make similar connections. I am a better person for knowing Gerry Nolan.

My hope, as you read this book, is the person behind it will come alive through these pages and inspire you to make connections. Continue those you have already made and discover the new ones that await.

~ Gayle Holte
Clinical Instructor, University of Wisconsin-Eau Claire, 2010-present
Elementary Principal, Fall Creek, Wisconsin, 2004-2010

A Note to the Reader

What Is Love?

*"Love is man's natural state, representing
our principle capacity to be human."*

~ Ashley Montagu

Giving and receiving love generously! This represents the highest nature of our being; the orientation to life through which we exercise our greatest influence. The more we nestle in this "natural state," the greater is our capacity to influence others in becoming fully actualized human beings.

What is love? What does it mean to be fully actualized? Before we explore the disposition, behaviors, and influence of loving teachers, we must define some parameters. The concept of love is so encompassing that no one definition sufficiently captures its depth or breadth (Sternberg and Barnes, 1988). We will thus identify common characteristics to guide our exploration, using the following definitions of love from a variety of perspectives.

- "Affectionate concern for the well-being of another" (Random House, 1993, p. 1139).

- "Unselfish, loyal and benevolent concern for the good of another" (Merriam-Webster, 1993, p. 690).

- "In theology: the feeling of benevolence and brotherhood that people should have for each other" (*Webster's New Twentieth Century Dictionary*, 1979, p. 870).

- "A complex yet basically unified emotion comprising tenderness, affection, and devotion to the well-being of another person or persons" (*The Encyclopedia of Human Behavior: Psychology, Psychiatry and Mental Health,* Goldenson, 1970, p. 108).

- Sociology: "In the social plane love is a meaningful interaction—or relationship—between two or more persons where the aspirations and aims of one person are shared and helped to their realization by other persons" (Sorokin, 1954, p. 13).

- Psychology: "A delight in the presence of the other person and an affirming of his value and development as much as one's own" (Dr. Rollo May, May 1953, p. 241).

- Psychiatry: "The will to extend one's self for the purpose of one's own or another's spiritual growth" (Peck, 1978, p. 94).

- "Love is patient, love is kind. It is not envious or boastful; it is not arrogant or rude. Love does not insist on its own way; it is not irritable or resentful; it does not rejoice in wrongdoing, but rejoices in the truth. Love bears all things, believes all things, hopes all things, endures all things. Love never fails" (1 Cor. 13:4-8).

- "Anything we do to help others discover their humanity. Any act where we turn to one another. Open our hearts. Extend ourselves. Listen. Any time we're patient. Curious. Quiet. Engaged" (Margaret Wheatley, 2002, p. 138).

LOVE AS A VERB

"Love ought to manifest itself in deeds rather than words."

~ St. Ignatius of Loyola

The common thread running through these definitions suggest that love is an orientation toward life and our fellow man: a relationship through which our actions are intended to promote the development and well-being of others. From this perspective, love is a verb denoting action, rather than a noun suggesting a feeling. Psychiatrist M. Scott Peck suggests that, "Genuine love is volitional rather than emotional" (Peck, 1978, p. 149). We demonstrate love by what we do, not how we feel. Love requires that we overcome our indifference and fear which are the antitheses of love. Acts of love are conscious choices willing to turn good intentions into actions. Quite simply, for Peck, "Love is as love does" (p. 97).

The ancient Greeks distinguished the three dimensions of love as Eros, Philia, and Agape. Eros refers to those things which bring us pleasure. When we say, "I love the opera…football…or a good meal," we are really saying that we enjoy these things because they bring us pleasure or eros. Philia, sometimes called brotherly love, refers to the affection or friendship we feel for others. We feel affection for a young child, a close friend, or even an endearing character in a movie. In both eros and philia, the pleasure we feel prevails. We are passive in this experience, and have yet to cross over into the active aspect of love, which is intended not for personal pleasure, but for the well-being of the other. Agape encompasses the active aspect of love. Agape includes the total acceptance of the other person as one who exists in their own right, while advancing the welfare and development of the other with no expectation of reciprocation (Hoyle, 2002; May, 1969; Kierkegaard, 1962; Fromm, 1956; Sorokin, 1954).

Credit Where Credit Is Due

"Teacherly love has the distinction of being both too obvious to study and too difficult to study. But it is too important to ignore."

~ Lisa Goldstein

To my knowledge, the term "Teacherly Love" was coined by Dr. Lisa Goldstein (1997) in her book, *Teaching with Love: A Feminist Approach to Early Childhood Education*. While not employing Goldstein's definition or conceptual underpinnings of Teacherly Love in this book, it is important to give Dr. Goldstein credit for a term that should grow in importance in our professional conversation.

Teacherly Love involves loving what we do (Eros), who we do it with (Philia), and who we do it for (Agape). Eros describes the pleasure we derive from teaching and helping students to realize their potential. Philia is the natural affection we feel for our students as members of the human family. I suggest Philia is an entry level disposition that all teachers must have. If we do not have affection for the students we serve, it will show. The students will know it, and their response to our efforts will be underwhelming. Agape is the other-centered love that compels us to go above and beyond expectations in the service of our students. Agape is the reason we come in early, stay late, and do whatever it takes to reach every student. Agape includes the sacrificial aspect of Teacherly Love, in which we often subordinate our own wants and needs in order to better serve our students.

Throughout this book you will encounter scores of definitions, descriptions, and comments regarding love. Each is correct in its own way but none of them on their own can capture the comprehensive nature or power of love. Please understand that it is with deep humility that, focused on the educational setting, we are taking on the single most important topic in the scope of human experience. This work is one voice among many that yearns to understand and express the essence of what it means to be a loving human being, or more accurately, a loving teacher.

Please consider the following definition of Teacherly Love, not as the Alpha and Omega on the subject, but as a succinct characterization on which this book is based. You will frequently encounter the terms employed in this definition as you progress through the book. It is the best I can offer, though it is inadequate to the scope and importance of the topic. I encourage you to develop your own definition which will act as a personal guide in directing your professional practice.

Teacherly Love is the awareness, willingness, and ability to nurture the goodness, well-being, and development of our students in the pursuit of truth, beauty, and goodness.

WHY LOVE?

"Love is, without any question, the most important experience
in the life of a human being."

~ Ashley Montagu

Renowned anthropologist and author Dr. Ashley Montagu came to the conclusion cited above only after examining the influence of love from a variety of scientific perspectives, including anthropology, sociology, biology, psychology, and the medical profession. His conclusion reflects the timeless nature of the human condition and the essential role that love plays in every aspect of human life. As educators we are in the human development business. This book is intended to examine the indispensable role that love plays in promoting the full, healthy development of our students. Love does not come from programs, text books, iPads, or any of the other tools we employ. Love only comes from fellow human beings. The love we demonstrate for our students—and the loving environment we create in our classrooms—is the most important factor in promoting student development. Everything presented in this book is based on this fundamental tenet of the human condition. We will demonstrate through research, personal experience, and the wisdom of master educators that love is the universal and timeless orientation to life that promotes human development. The most effective teachers are loving teachers.

For thousands of years human beings have learned from one another through imitation, shared experience, and seeing the world through each other's eyes. As mammals, as the ultimate herd animals, the love we have for one another, the selfless acts that promote the goodness, well-being and development of our fellow man, has allowed us to prosper, grow, and indeed survive as a species. Great teachers employ these same practices to promote the well-being and development of the students they serve.

In this work, you will encounter insights regarding the power of love from great thinkers in the areas of science, philosophy, education, and religion. There is significant agreement as to what love is, how we communicate our love, and the benefits that naturally flow to both the giver and receiver of love.

You will encounter the wisdom of loving teachers as they describe the orientation of love that informs their professional practice. My hope is that you will be inspired, challenged, and affirmed through these insights. I am confident you will see your own wisdom reflected in their words.

You will encounter the beauty of loving teachers as they describe the behaviors that are part of their professional practice. Through their insights and stories I believe you will identify your own beauty as a loving teacher.

Through the insights of both teachers and students you will witness the blessings which naturally flow from love shared. From a big picture perspective these blessings manifest themselves in three main areas, by promoting the goodness, well-being, and development of our students. We have all said something like, "He's such a good kid." What we are really saying is that the student has a good heart and a great capacity to love. When students feel loved they reciprocate that love and pass it on to others. The goodness that we witness is just that: an increased capacity to love. Students' well-being is a natural byproduct of being loved, valued, and affirmed. Development includes every aspect of our nature, mind, heart, body, and spirit. Love drives out the fear that inhibits development, creating the conditions where every student is free to be themselves and develop the gifts they possess. My hope is that you will be affirmed in your own professional practice through the stories and insights of fellow educators.

If you are skeptical about this premise—that love is the indispensable element promoting human development in our schools—you are not alone. I was too, but I was dragged to this conclusion, kicking and screaming. I encourage you to read this with an open mind and an open heart. Both will be required. If your orientation to teaching is already reflected in this premise, then you will be affirmed, challenged, and encouraged to spread the good news.

You will be introduced to Coach Darold Andrist, my champion and a most influential teacher whose unconditional love powerfully influenced my development. He remains a guiding influence in my life today. My hope is that through these descriptions you will see a reflection of your own influence with the students whom you teach and love.

You will encounter the Dark Side: an occasional glimpse into what happens when love is absent in the student-teacher relationship. The purpose is not to wallow in heartbreak, but to understand what to avoid. Anthony de Mello wrote in *Awareness: The Perils and Opportunities of Reality*, that "Love cannot be defined; unlove can. Drop unlove, drop fear, and you will know" (1990, p. 98). To define or even describe love is a very delicate matter. It is sometimes more useful to describe "unlove" as a means to understand what love is. Because we are hard-wired to give and receive love, when we drop "unlove," love naturally occurs.

It Begins With Us

"Love given unconditionally reflects the highest nature of our species."

~ Abraham Maslow

Make no mistake: bringing our highest self, our love, into the classroom every day, is not an easy task. While our nature seeks to give and receive love, we also possess an ego and survival instincts that often conflict with our willingness and ability to love. Nevertheless, through will and courage we can live our highest nature, providing students with what they need most. Abraham Maslow suggests that love is the most important agent promoting full actualization. Fellow educator Leo Buscaglia described love as the ultimate behavior modifier. Truly, love is the most important experience we can offer our students in their path to full, healthy human development.

TEACHING, BY ITS NATURE, IS AN ACT OF LOVE

"Love is the relationship between persons which contributes to the welfare and development of each."

~ Ashley Montagu

Of the many definitions and descriptions of love that have been written, I find Dr. Ashley Montagu's the most serviceable for its simplicity and truthfulness. Every discussion of love is founded on a relationship that is ultimately mutually beneficial. It is not a quid pro quo reflecting conditional love, but a natural phenomenon growing out of a commitment to contribute to the welfare and development of the beloved.

I suggest that teaching, by its nature, is an act of love. Please re-read Dr. Montagu's statement while substituting the word "teaching" for "love." Would you agree that this is an accurate description of what it means to be a teacher: to contribute to the welfare and development of our students? Would you also agree that when we promote our students' welfare and development, that we naturally enrich our own lives? At its core, teaching is an act of love. Great teachers are great because of their capacity to love.

ROOT CHALLENGES

"There are a thousand hacking at the branches of evil to one who is striking at the root."

~ Henry David Thoreau

I often begin my presentations throughout the country by asking participants to describe the traits of the people—mainly teachers—who exercised the greatest influence in their lives. The answers are pretty much the same with every group. "They believed in me"; "They cared about me"; "They had high expectations for me"; "They never quit on me"; "They gave me confidence in myself"; and, "They were kind, especially when I needed that." Every group describes the action of a loving human being. No one has ever said, "I was so grateful that Mr. Peterson used the McGraw-Hill math program," or, "Using iPads changed my entire outlook on life," or, "I would never be where I am now if Mrs. Smith hadn't taught us the six plus one writing traits system." Programs, pedagogy, and gizmos are all negotiable, as there are a lot of serviceable methods and programs on the market. Acts of love provided through the human element—classroom teachers—are non-negotiable in promoting full, healthy, human development. If you get nothing else out of this work, I hope you will view teaching as an act of love. Let's look at some root problems in the educational system that can only be addressed successfully through the human element, grounded in love.

The state of American education is largely measured through high stakes testing. Test scores in themselves are not inherently problematic, but their applications may be. They do tell us something about the state of education in America, but an increasing number of educators are becoming skeptical about how well they reveal the efficacy of our schools. Basic "root" issues that heavily influence poor test results have for the most part been ignored or glossed over. Until and unless these basic issues are addressed there will be no significant change nationally in standardized test results.

According to a survey of nearly 150,000 sixth through twelfth grade students in 202 communities across the country, only 29% indicated that they experienced a caring school climate (Scales and Leffert, 2004). Scales and Leffert define a caring teacher as one who is considered fair but who also has high expectations for student behavior and academic excellence. They are also friendly, approachable, and have a genuine concern for all students. Students who feel cared for are respected and valued as contributing members of their class.

If you were a student who didn't believe any of the teachers cared about you, how much effort would you put into a standardized test? High school students understand that the only test that will make any personal difference to them is a college entrance exam such as the ACT or SAT. State level standardized tests mean little to nothing to most high school students. Students who feel cared for—feel loved—will perform well because they don't want to let their teachers down. If only 29% of the students feel cared for in our schools, it is reasonable to assume that the rest won't give their best efforts on a test that means nothing to them. I submit that low test scores are more of an indication of the state of the poor relationships in our schools, rather than being an accurate reflection of the efficacy of the educational programs.

The national graduation rate is just under 75% (Diploma Counts, 2015). While the graduation rate has increased in recent years, this number sadly indicates that 25% of the students who enter high school walk out our doors prior to graduation. The drop-out rate is even higher than 25%, because students who drop out prior to entering high school do not show up in the dropout data. Approximately 1 million students each year leave our schools having not earned a high school diploma. This equates to about 5,500 students dropping out each day that our schools are in session. The personal and societal damage caused by this waste of human poten-tial is inestimable and heartbreaking. It is a national tragedy that takes place one student at a time. I suggest we can best address this heartbreak through loving student-teacher relationships. Ackerman (1997) reports that the most important factor preventing students from dropping out of school is the presence of just one interested adult in the life of a student.

We also face other challenges originating from society at large. Daniel Goleman (1995) tells us that, "On average, children are growing more lonely and depressed, more angry and unruly, more nervous and prone to worry, more impulsive and aggressive." My own experience in education for over thirty years suggests that this statement is true. Each of these conditions is a major impediment to actualizing potential.

A Solution

"The learning for all of us seems clear. If power is the capacity generated by our relationships, then we need to be attending to the quality of those relationships. We would do well to ponder the realization that love is the most potent source of power."

~ Margaret Wheatley

Many of our students come to us with what might be described as a "love deficit." In *The Art of Loving,* Erich Fromm suggests that very few have ever experienced a truly loving relationship. Gary Chapman in *The Five Love Languages* describes this tendency as having an empty love tank. Many students simply do not, for a variety of reasons, experience an adequate level of love in their lives. Would students who experience love and belonging in our schools walk out our doors by the millions? Love is the natural antidote to loneliness, anxiety, and aggression. Students who are at peace, who feel connected to significant others, who are comfortable in their own skins, and who do not experience fear and anxiety are prepared to learn. These conditions cannot be addressed by programs, pedagogy, or gizmos. Our natures demand love, which can only be provided by a fellow human being, as the cure for the maladies of loneliness, anxiety, depression, and anger. This means that you and I are the solution to these root problems that plague both schools and society.

The solution does not lie in more money, a new math or reading program, one-to-one computing, or any other *thing* we can throw at these issues. Things are not patient, kind, or understanding. Things don't see the gifts that each student possesses. Things don't communicate to students their value and potential so that they come to see it in themselves. Things don't help reluctant learners say "yes" to life and learning. Only you and I, as the fellow human beings in our classrooms, can supply these and other acts of love to address these issues. The resiliency literature is replete with evidence suggesting that the human element is the most important protective factor influencing "at-risk" students who transcend the impediments in their lives. Werner and Smith (1992) reported that, "The resilient youngsters in our study all had at least one person accept them unconditionally regardless of temperamental idiosyncrasies, physical attractiveness, or intelligence" (p. 205). Because we want students to feel cared for, because we want to stop the stampede of students out of our schools, and because we want students to experience community instead of loneliness, happiness instead of depression, peace instead of anxiety, we must look to love—our love—as the solution to these problems. When students feel cared for, when they stay in our classrooms, when anxiety is replaced with peace of mind, then and only then will the high stakes test scores improve dramatically. Student after student I have interviewed has stated that they would never let a teacher down who they felt was in their corner and loved them. One of the blessings of Teacherly Love is that all human beings will perform for those they love (Fay and Funk, 1995). One way students exhibit love for their teachers is through their performance. When we cultivate our true nature, understanding that love is, without any question, the most important experience in the life of every human being, we will realize the full potential of every student we serve and will have the schools that we all dream about.

THIS IS NOT A FORMULA

"Truth cannot be put into words, into a formula. That isn't the truth. That isn't reality. Reality cannot be put into a formula."

~ Anthony de Mello

There is no one formula for loving behavior just as there is no one effective way to teach. While this book is organized around three main themes, this is not intended to limit what it means to be a loving teacher. It merely suggests that these are ways in which teachers can and do express love for their students.

I simply offer a point of view for your consideration. I challenge you to make your own examination of the nature of the human condition while considering the role that love plays in promoting full, healthy human development. Then draw your own conclusions and develop your own applications that reflect your unique nature as a member of the human family.

> *"The most effective and most accessible way to acquire the maximum of constructive power is to love truly and wisely."*
>
> ~ Pitirim Sorokin

Personal Prologue:
The Tale of Two Teachers

*"The most important influence for good in my life have been
my teachers, and any good that I may have done or may yet do
in the world will be due largely, if not entirely,
to the influence of my teachers."*

~ Ashley Montagu

I have been blessed with many great teachers who completely gave of themselves for my welfare and development. I suspect you have had the same experience. Never doubt that you exercise this same influence for the students you serve. The most influential in my life was Coach Darold Andrist. Coach Andrist arrived in Weyauwega, Wisconsin, as a student teacher sometime during the middle of my sixth grade year. I could never have imagined the profound impact he would have on my life, and his influence endures to this day.

This story illustrates the three connections of Teacherly Love around which this book is organized. These connections do not operate in isolation; they support, reinforce, and illuminate each other. Because Coach Andrist knew and understood me personally, he was equipped to work with me professionally. Because he identified and communicated the potential he saw in me, we shared a vision that continues to be a compelling force in my life. Because he met me where I was developmentally, he was able to coach me through my limitations while emphasizing my strengths. Because he expected so much of himself, I was willing to accept the high expectations he had for me. Because he respected me as a unique individual, I respected him. Because of his kindness, I was able to overcome short-term disappointments without falling into despair. Because he freely shared his time and expertise, I was willing to accept his coaching, criticism, and counsel. Because of his genuine enthusiasm for life, he remains for me a real model of what it means to live life fully. Because there was no doubt in my mind that he was unconditionally in my corner, there was nothing I would not do for him. During the seven years that Coach was such an influential part of my life, I would not have described all the things he did for me as acts of love. Looking back, I cannot describe them in any other way. The defining characteristic of Coach Andrist's professional practice was the love that he shared with all of his students and athletes. Through the influence of his love, I grew in every dimension of my life, am at peace with who I am, and continue to work toward realizing my full potential.

My Champion

"Champion: A person who fights for or defends any person or cause."
~ Random House Dictionary

Coach Andrist championed my development as a young adult, but my experience was not unique, for he developed this relationship with every student and athlete he served. While our professional relationship was that of a coach and student-athlete, it would be insufficient to characterize our relationship strictly within those parameters. Coach Andrist was a mentor, counselor, and life skills coach. As I grew older we became good friends. No other adult exercised a greater influence in my life, except my parents, Marie and Dave Nolan.

Among the many blessings I derived from our relationship, he shared three important and enduring gifts: a vision of accomplishment which drove me to push the boundaries of abilities (personal connection), high expectations in every aspect of my life (professional connection), and being a real model whom I wished to emulate (charismatic connection).

Our identities as young adults are profoundly influenced through the social mirror. If we are told that we are smart, insightful, and capable, we tend to believe and manifest these attributes.

Dr. Stephen R. Covey, in his book *The 8th Habit* (2004), defined leadership this way: "communicating to others their worth and potential so clearly that they come to see it in themselves" (p. 98). Through Coach's influence I embraced a vision for myself that went well beyond my role as a student-athlete. The fact that I am writing this book is a manifestation of the worth and potential that I continue to realize in my life.

I was drawn to my potential as a wrestler through Coach's influence. He saw in me the potential to be a state champion. This vision strongly guided, indeed dominated, my life for many years. The vision was vivid, inspiring, and never far from my consciousness. If I had a mission statement as a young man it would have been: "Do everything in my power to develop the strength, skills, and mindset to become a state wrestling champion." And yet for Coach Andrist, becoming a state champion was not the end: it was the means. Wrestling was the vehicle through which he taught important life lessons which endured well beyond my wrestling career.

Coach is a "real model." Many suggest that students need role models. I disagree. What our students need are *real* models: adults who model lives of integrity, not duplicity. Sadly, too often in our society style trumps substance, making duplicity attractive and integrity quaint. Young people have had too many fake role models, adults preaching one thing while doing another. Many students' lives are full of duplicitous adults acting the part but never really being themselves.

With Coach Andrist, what you see is what you get. There is nothing phony or contrived about him. Being a genuinely caring and loving teacher isn't about having a repertoire of techniques that one can pull out of a hat when necessary. It is about integrity as the core of our being, genuinely representing who we are. Coach Andrist exemplifies this type of teacher. His other attributes include enthusiasm, understanding, respect, a great sense of humor, inquisitiveness, kindness, consideration, belief in others, forgiveness, patience, and a tenacious work ethic. He has a ready smile, an infectious laugh, and that unique ability to put others at ease. Accomplished in a number of areas, he is always humble and generous with his time. As a real model, Coach Andrist is as good as it gets.

Coach had extraordinarily high expectations for all of his student-athletes. This included a duty to develop our gifts in every aspect of our lives; mind, heart, body and spirit. Wrestling was the vehicle through which Coach influenced the development of his student-athletes. Being successful wrestlers was not enough. He expected us to be great students, devoted sons and daughters, positive real models for our team and younger student-athletes, and to develop a vision for our lives while being willing to pay the price to realize those visions. Coach emphasized our responsibility to develop these gifts for our own advantage as well as to benefit others. He educated the "whole child" long before it became a catch phrase.

It is common for people to fondly describe a teacher who pushed them to high achievement. With Coach Andrist, it always felt like co-participation. He not so much pushed me but worked beside me, like we were in it together. If I succeeded, he succeeded. If I failed, he failed. We were truly a team. It was easy to have high expectations for myself when I had a mentor who had the same expectations for himself. I am humbled to recall the support Coach Andrist provided me as a young man. He supported my development particularly in three ways, all of which are attributes of great teachers.

1. Coach Andrist was very knowledgeable, always staying current in the sport. He attended every available wrestling clinic, continually adding to his knowledge base and expertise, and when possible he took some of the team with him. Coach always prepared me to win because he paid the price by developing his own knowledge and skills. The execution was up to me.

2. Coach Andrist gave me real models to emulate. He took me to watch the best wrestlers at the state wrestling tournament when I was in junior high and at collegiate national tournaments when I was in high school. We even went to the Olympic trials to witness some of the best wrestlers in the world. This gave me the opportunity to observe how real champions competed.

3. Coach Andrist committed the time in preparing me to realize the vision of becoming a state champion. This included wrestling with me nearly every day during the summers of my high school years. One of the enduring lessons I learned from Coach was the commitment of time and effort to be the best.

These attributes are all examples of what outstanding teachers regularly do. Some see the roles of teacher and coach as somehow different, almost as being at odds with one another. I never have. Being an effective coach involves the same orientation and skill-set as being an effective teacher. We have to love what we are doing, love who we are doing it with, and love those for whom we are doing it. This applies to the kindergarten teacher, the high school physics teacher, the college professor, or the high school wrestling coach.

Like every adolescent, I experienced numerous setbacks in various areas of my life, including wrestling. On more than one occasion I was ready to throw in the towel. Resiliency was not one of my strengths, but I was fortunate to have a coach who embodied resilience. We learn from literature on this subject that oftentimes the difference between despair and hope is one loving adult who can help us imagine, plan, and realize a more promising future (Werner and Smith, 1992). Persistence is one of Coach Andrist's greatest attributes. He never gave up on me even when I had given up on myself.

My first interactions with him were fairly sporadic as we only had physical education class a couple of times per week. Initial impressions were favorable because he was the first physical education teacher I had who was consistently friendly, supportive, and enthusiastic. Predictably, everyone looked forward to his class. His enthusiasm breathed new life into what had previously been a rather sterile experience. His personable manner brought out the best in each student. He was always patient, willing to take extra time to provide every student with the help they needed to develop their skills. He asked thoughtful questions that encouraged us to coach ourselves. He was patient in answering our questions—even if it was the same question that had been asked five seconds before. He fundamentally changed our physical education experience by exposing us to a variety of fun and challenging activities.

Within a few months of his arrival, he had convinced my classmates and me that we were all gifted in some way. Being of average size, speed, and strength, I can assure you I was not very talented. But that didn't seem to matter to him, so it didn't matter to me. I saw myself as he saw me: someone special who had the potential to develop extraordinary abilities. This was his greatest gift to me: he saw talents and abilities in me that I had never seen in myself. His orientation of love allowed him to look past the frailties, limitations, and insecurities of my youth, to see potential that was grander than I could envision for myself.

He was the first physical education teacher who took the time to test all of us for the Presidential Physical Fitness Award. He was determined to help as many of us as possible to earn that blue patch. For those who really wanted to excel, he voluntarily set up training times after school. He wanted us to succeed even more than we did ourselves.

I really needed to work on my strength for the pull-ups and my speed for the sixty-yard dash. He gave us great tips on how to train and perform and be successful. He noticed that I was not very fast, so I needed help with my start. When you're not naturally fast you need an explosive start to have any chance of success. He understood my weakness but was able to focus on my strength—my quickness—to give me my best chance of success. Because he knew and understood me as an individual, he was equipped to help me capitalize on my strengths while compensating for my limitations.

Many of us qualified for the Presidential Physical Fitness Award. I still remember the pride of accomplishment we felt when we received those blue patches. The single most important factor in our accomplishment of this goal was the loving service of one teacher, Mr. Darold Andrist. While the Presidential patch was important then, there are lessons from that experience that are more important in my life. I still ponder today as an educator the concept that we are called to bring out the best in each other. As teachers we have the opportunity to do this every day. We are best able to accomplish this task through an orientation of loving service.

One of the fruits of love is a positive outlook, a zest for life. Coach Andrist is the most optimistic person I know. No one can be universally optimistic without being full of love. I never heard anyone—and I mean anyone—say a bad thing about Mr. Andrist. He was universally loved and respected because he universally loved and respected others. He remains my Champion.

THE DARK SIDE

*"Everyone is a moon, and has a dark side
which he never shows to anybody."*

~ Mark Twain

Hatred, fear, and indifference are widely accepted as love's opposites. If we hate our jobs, use fear as our primary motivational scheme, or are indifferent to the development of students, we operate from the Dark Side. The Dark Side is characterized by a lack of love or an abundance of unlove. When unlove is present, the damage inflicted on everyone involved, especially ourselves, is unfortunate and avoidable. The reason for examining unlove is that it tells us clearly what not to do. When we steer clear of unlove we do no harm, which may be the best we can hope for in some situations.

While I had many great teachers, I also had a few clunkers along the way. I suppose we all do. These teachers made me wonder why they chose our profession. Few though they may be, these teachers are bad for our profession and for kids. The following is my experience with a teacher who exhibited a total absence of love for his students and his profession, while exhibiting all three facets which I believe make up the Dark Side: hatred, fear and indifference.

As a freshman in high school my vocational education teacher nicknamed me "Pinhead." I'm not sure how I earned this moniker, but "Hey, Pinhead," was the insulting greeting I received every day upon entering class. This derogatory nickname was one of many manifestations of this teacher's decidedly unloving orientation to his work and students. "Darth Vader" treated all of his students in a similar fashion. It seemed to be his nature. Just as I tried to live up to Coach Andrist's high expectations, I did my best to live down to Mr. Vader's label of "Pinhead." Thankfully, I had many loving and supportive adults in my life so I never took Mr. Vader's view of me too seriously. He was not one of the voices that resonated through my social mirror. Nevertheless, it is sad to consider the negative impact he had on many students who lacked the validation of a loving support system. Mr. Vader hated teaching and he hated the kids, consequently he was never happy in his work and his students never flourished.

Fear was Mr. Vader's classroom management tool of choice as he attempted to intimidate his students by playing the tough guy. His act was not convincing because deep down he was scared to death and everyone knew it. Like most teachers who use fear as their main source of influence, when the source of that fear, the teacher, is out of sight, chaos can occur. Conversely, no one would ever have thought to let Coach Andrist down by misbehaving, whether he was present or not. There were upwards of thirty wrestlers and cheerleaders at every tournament yet no one ever considered getting into mischief. None of us would ever disappoint Coach Andrist in that way. Love has an enduring, far reaching influence that fear does not. The use of fear as a behavior modifier is seductive because its influence is immediate. Long term influence is the province of love.

Another downside of using fear in the classroom is that fear is the great inhibitor, engendering doubt and blinding us to our potential. While love is characterized by an abundance mentality in which all of life's prospects are evident, fear injects a scarcity mentality limiting our vision and optimism. When experiencing high levels of anxiety, including fear, we encounter what Goleman (1995) describes as "emotional hijacking." These highly emotionalized states interfere with functions of the neo-cortex and inhibit effective use of short-term memory. Goleman suggests that this is why "continual emotional distress can create deficits in a child's intellectual abilities, crippling the capacity to learn" (1995, p. 27). Conversely, being in a good mood enhances the ability to think clearly and problem solve. Laughing and joking enhance critical thinking and problem-solving skills as the mind is more predisposed to look at alternatives from a constructive perspective (Goleman, 1995).

Perhaps the most malignant antithesis of love is unbridled indifference. Through indifference one becomes a cipher, not rising to the level of deserving hatred or the significance of being manipulated by fear. To an indifferent person, one simply doesn't matter. This was the relationship Mr. Vader cultivated with most of his students. I was in class every day, but it would have been all the same to him if I had been a trained seal or a banana tree. The result was predictable. Because Mr. Vader was indifferent toward his students, they responded with unrestrained apathy toward his class. I have never been a part of a class where so little was expected or accomplished. Thankfully, he was relieved of his professional duties a few years later.

Mr. Vader and Coach Andrist were polar opposites. The wisdom and beauty exhibited by Coach Andrist were totally foreign concepts to Mr. Vader. Coach Andrist loved his job and his students. For reasons that we cannot know, Mr. Vader did not love either, or perhaps, he was sadly unaware of how to communicate his compassion for his students. Love is a learned behavior. Perhaps Mr. Vader never had a model of Teacherly Love to follow.

There was one striking similarity between the two. Each received, in exact one-to-one proportion, what he gave to his students. Coach Andrist was universally loved and respected because he exhibited nothing but love and respect. Darth was universally despised because he despised his students and his job. Mr. Andrist had a long history of effectiveness as both a teacher and coach. Darth Vader had a mercifully short career, contributing nothing of value to his students or his profession. The difference between the two was quite simple. Coach Andrist operated out of love, while Mr. Vader operated within the prison of unlove.

"Love cannot be defined; unlove can.
Drop unlove, drop fear, and you will know."

~ Anthony de Mello

PART I

Personal Connection

PART I

....

Personal Connection

"Love implies the possession of a feeling of deep involvement in another, and to love another means to communicate that feeling of involvement with him."

~ Ashley Montagu

While we divide Teacherly Love into three domains: the personal, professional, and charismatic connections, each domain informs, illuminates, and supports the others. The interplay is more like an ecosystem than three silos that house distinctive characteristics separately. For example, knowing a student well (personal connection) provides insights that will inform how to best approach each student through the professional connection. Our enthusiasm (charismatic connection) illuminates the importance of what we are teaching through the professional connection. Our kindness (personal connection) is a key factor in creating an environment conducive to learning (professional connection). Having an outstanding knowledge base (professional connection) is often a gateway to personal connection with students who share similar interests. Effectiveness in any one area creates opportunities for connection in other areas.

The personal connection is, in a sense, the purest connection because it involves the basic communion of one human being with another. It transcends the positional relationship of teacher to student, reflecting an organic, human-to-human relationship. Because it is the most basic connection, one could argue it is the most important because through the personal connection we first capture the hearts of our students. According to Beishuizen, Hof, Von Putten, Bouw-meester and Asscher (2001), secondary teachers cited the relation-ship with the student as their top priority, while secondary students also emphasized the relationship aspects of effective teachers as being more important than the transfer of knowledge and skills. We suggest that the transfer of knowledge and skills is often mediated through the more foundational personal connection. The maxim, "Students don't care how much we know until they know how much we care," applies.

If a football team cannot perform the basic skills of blocking, tackling, and hanging on to the ball, they will be unsuccessful despite the schemes they run. If they block and tackle and hang on to the ball, then almost any scheme will do. When we develop person-to-person relationships with our students, we are mastering the basics of what it means to be an effective educator, laying the foundation for teaching knowledge and skills. For this reason we begin with the basics, the blocking and tackling of teaching: the personal connec-tion.

Psychologists tell us that as much as 85% of the joy and satis-faction we derive from life is based on the quality of our relation-ships. The opposite is also true. When our relationships are poor, our overall satisfaction with life suffers. Students who develop positive relationships with their teachers and classmates are more engaged in school, reach higher levels of achievement, and experience greater satisfaction with school. In short, "Children who feel better about school do better in school" (Starkman, Scales and Roberts, 1999, p. 2).

If you have children of your own, I am confident that you have had a conversation that went something like this:

"How is school going, Jimmy?"
"Great, Dad. I really like school this year."
"Why is that?"
"I really like Mrs. Finnegan. She is really cool."

Rarely is there mention of the subject taught by the teacher because it is the relationship with the teacher that matters most. As a parent you may also have had a conversation that was just the opposite. Your child does not like math because they don't like the teacher. Aspey and Roebuck (1977) conducted studies with more than 500 teachers and over 10,000 students on behalf of the National Consortium for Humanizing Education. The title of their book represents their major finding, *Kids Don't Learn from People They Don't Like.* The personal connections we develop with students are the foundation for learning.

Rogers (1983) suggests that we do not really teach students anything; we can only facilitate learning. The important facilitative conditions are not books, audio-visual aids, techniques or even the content knowledge of the teacher. Rogers suggests, "No, the facilitation of significant learning rests upon certain attitudinal qualities that exist in the personal relationship between the facilitator and the learner" (Rogers, 1983, p. 121). The most important frame of reference indicating whether or not school is "good" is the relationship your child has with their teachers.

The importance of the personal connection happens at every level of education. For my own children this pattern was consistent all the way through college. Our oldest daughter began college as a print journalism major but graduated as a geography major, minoring in literature. The geography major was a complete surprise to everyone. The initial step down this path was the relationship she developed with some of the geography professors. These relationships began on the personal level and then developed into professional relationships that opened doors she could not anticipate, including several trips to Turkey and other countries in the Middle East. Consider your own career path and how much your journey was influenced by the relationships you developed with key teachers and mentors along the way. The quality of our relationships influences our identity, satisfaction, and path in life.

Anna, a student, described the importance of the personal connection this way:

> I think for me it makes me more interested in the subject that they are teaching. I hated trig last year because I didn't get along with Mr. Skaags. But then this year I got to talking with him more and we hit it off and I got more interested in trig because I could relate to it better. I guess

that was because I could relate better to Mr. Skaags. Like this morning in trig, Mr. Skaags asked what was going on with track and what happened with softball. And since I'm not in athletics he asked me what happened with the cadaver. He knew we had taken a trip to see a cadaver at the university. So that was cool, since I am kind of the odd duck out in that class anyways. So he finds ways to draw me in.

Anna experienced success in trigonometry, not because Mr. Skaags changed his teaching style, or because the school adopted a new math program. No, Anna's success happened, "because I could relate better to Mr. Skaags," because "he finds ways to draw me in." Anna, after having failed trig the previous year, experienced success because of her personal connection to Mr. Skaags. This story is repeated thousands of times every day in our schools. It reflects our common nature as the ultimate herd animal as well as our need for psychological intimacy with other human beings (Maslow, 1971).

Peter echoed the sentiments of many students when he shared, "Like the classes that I've been in where the teacher just stands up front for forty-five minutes and lectures, it just seems to have less effect. Like if you spend the first couple minutes talking about your day before they get you going, even with a little less time you will still get a lot more out of it." Any time committed to developing the personal connection is time well spent, paying dividends in promoting both quality relationships and enhanced achievement.

Mr. Hinsdale, a master social studies teacher, offers this advice about the personal connection.

As a teacher, one of the things you need to do is like students. If you like everything else but you don't like teenagers, then don't go into the business. Don't do it for the contract. I have 138 students during the day. They are 138 unique individuals. You really have to like students and you have to deal with everything that is going on in their lives because you never know what's going to happen in your classroom that day. You have to be able to deal with it: good, bad or indifferent.

The experiences of Anna and Peter support the notion that a personal connection is important to learning. Their intuition is backed by neuroscience which affirms the importance of the personal connection in promoting full, healthy human development. Siegel (1999) observes that relationship experiences have a dominant influence on brain development because the circuits responsible for social perception are tightly linked to those that integrate the creation of meaning, regulation of body states, modulation of emotion, organization of memory, and capacity for interpersonal communication. Interpersonal experience thus plays a special organizing role in determining the development of brain structure early in life and the ongoing emergence of brain function throughout the lifespan.

Interpersonal interaction is important to the effective creation, engagement, and refinement of neural networks at any age. The sensory and cognitive stimulation received through prolonged interpersonal relationships with parents and other adults is especially important to the development of a child's brain and intelligence capacity. Brain development is particularly responsive to social intimacies of touch, voice, facial expression, and shared thoughts. In fact, direct social interaction with other humans is the primary means by which we develop, maintain, and adjust our emotional and cognitive competencies throughout our lifetime. Simply put, social interaction is what the brain expects and depends on—as the lungs expect and depend on oxygen to perform their function. The brain is designed to interact with other human brains. Social interaction in childhood, moreover, is the essential vehicle by which we construct meaning for our physical and biological world, sense of self, and moral and cultural orientation (Dickmann and Stanford-Blair, 2002).

There is a misconception in our profession which suggests that all we need to do is apply certain research based teaching techniques and we all become master teachers. Applying the science of teaching and learning is certainly important, but we must also master the art of teaching, which, by its nature, requires a person-to-person relationship. I submit to you the art of teaching is far more difficult to master than the science. Expecting well-informed technocrats in the science of teaching who are unable to build relationships with students to become effective teachers runs counter to our human nature. We must emphasize the importance of the student-teacher relationship while recognizing that, in order to be effective, the basis of that relationship must be love. Wheatley (1999) suggests that our relationships must be based on love. "The learning for all of us seems clear. If power is the capacity generated by our relationships, then we need to be attending to the quality of those relationships. We would do well to ponder the realization that love is the most potent source of power" (Wheatley, 1999, p. 40).

Because our goal is to facilitate student development, we must commit ourselves to demonstrating love for our students every day through a personal connection. Through love we offer the opportunity for each student to discover and refine the gifts they possess. In successful interpersonal relationships there is "a dimly sensed recognition that the strongest force in our universe is not overriding power, but love" (Rogers, 1980, p. 204).

As you read the following three chapters, I hope you will reflect on the myriad opportunities we have to build effective and meaningful relationships with our students through the power of love. Through these relationships we not only make learning a more satisfying experience, we also open the door to the academic development of each student, which lies at the core of our professional journey. "Students who feel supported (loved, affirmed and accepted) feel that they are connected to people they value and that adults know them and care for them. They also feel that they have adults that they can turn to for help of various kinds, such as dealing with emotional problems, learning new skills, or obtaining financial resources" (Scales and Leffert, 2004, pp. 22-23).

"All the evidence bearing upon this matter with which I am acquainted suggests that there is one word which better than any other indicates what love really is. That word is interdependence."

~ Ashley Montagu

Chapter One:
Know Our Students Well

WHY KNOWING OUR STUDENTS WELL IS LOVE AND WHY IT MATTERS

"To respect a person is not possible without knowing him: care and responsibility would be blind if it were not guided by knowledge. Knowledge would be empty if it were not motivated by concern. There are many layers of knowledge; the knowledge which is an aspect of love is one which does not stay on the periphery, but penetrates the core."

~ Erich Fromm

A wide variety of literature suggests that love is communicated through taking an active interest in knowing the beloved well. Similarly, educational literature suggests that effective teachers take an active interest in getting to know their students well. Learning each student's life story requires awareness, patience, empathy, and a willingness to listen, all of which are elements of love. Understanding the uniqueness of each student's story equips us to lovingly meet their individual needs.

One of our greatest needs is to be known as individuals possessing talents, aspirations, and perspectives that are uniquely our own. Indeed, we are born with a yearning for psychological intimacy with other human beings (Maslow, 1971). We overcome the sense of isolation that lies at the root of all anxiety by being known. Ashley Montagu (1953) suggests that "Man was born for participation, and there is no pain more unbearable than the feeling of being alone" (p. 11). We scale this wall of isolation by expressing interest in the lives of our students. We thereby provide the loving security that meets each student's basic need for attunement and psychological intimacy, which in turn fuels human development.

Human capacity for learning expects and depends on rich social interaction (Greenough, Black, & Wallace, 1987). The brain expects and depends on relationships with its environment, particularly interpersonal relationships, to realize its potential. It requires a social unfolding of its genetic program. In effect, "human connections shape the neural connections from which the mind emerges" (Siegel, 1999). Interacting with students on a personal level provides the social experience which is the great initiator of thinking and learning (Dickmann and Stanford-Blair, 2002). The following stories illustrate how knowing our students well is a mutually beneficial act of love, which enhances learning.

I HATE THIS PLACE

"To be in the state called love you must be sensitive to the uniqueness and beauty of every single living thing and person."

~ Anthony de Mello

Jill was a second semester senior in Mr. Blake's high school American Government class. For several days in a row, Jill paused as she was about to leave the classroom and said, "I hate this place." Jill did not say this directly to Mr. Blake, but spoke loudly enough to make sure he would hear it. While Mr. Blake didn't know Jill well, he was concerned for her well-being and didn't want any student to feel this way about school. The next day, Mr. Blake positioned himself by the door to intercept Jill before she could make her patented get-away. Jill repeated her exiting remark, but this time Mr. Blake stopped her and asked, "Do you really hate this place?"

Mr. Blake described Jill's response this way:

"Well no, but…" and then she gets it out and stands there and talks to me for twenty minutes. I listened to everything she had to say but I don't think she cared if I heard one bit of it. She just had to get it off her chest and it was done. As she was talking, her whole countenance changed. As she shared her story she decompressed physically and emotionally. When she finished she was totally at ease. And when she left she had the biggest smile on her face and she said, "You know what? I don't hate this place at all. I just have trouble with some of the people who are around me sometimes and I don't like certain situations that I have to deal with."

It would have been easy for Mr. Blake to blow off Jill's comments as a symptom of senioritis or typical high school drama. Thankfully Mr. Blake showed the courage and compassion to get involved. He showed compassion because he sensed a need and acted, and courage because there was no way of knowing how Jill would respond when he asked the simple question. Most importantly, he just listened. Jill didn't need him to say anything; she just needed an ear to bend and Mr. Blake obliged.

The blessings that emerged for both Jill and Mr. Blake developed over time. The class ended right before lunch each day so Jill began to stay after class for a few minutes to shoot the breeze. Mr. Blake became a sounding board and mentor for Jill. As deadlines for college applications approached, Mr. Blake wrote an outstanding letter of recommendation that Jill cherished and which helped her get accepted to the college of her choice. Small acts of love like noticing, asking, and listening can lead to a meaningful relationship, which in this case, enriched the lives of both Jill and Mr. Blake.

IT's A FAMILY AFFAIR

"The simplest way to begin finding each other again is to start talking about what we care about."

~ Margaret Wheatley

The most natural, meaningful, and interesting topics of discussion for most people are themselves or their families. Loving teachers capitalize on this facet of the human psyche to make a personal connection. High school student Kim enthusiastically shared the following experience:

> In second grade I went to the Opportunity School where the whole curriculum was based on families, working together with other kids, and it was more hands-on. So our teachers got really involved with our families. Every year as part of our family tradition my family celebrates with a Japanese New Year party. My teacher was aware of that, so she put that extra effort out. She wanted to learn more about our family celebration and made it into a class event. My mom and dad worked with her and we had our Japanese New Year party at school with all my classmates. Doing things like this helped her better understand her kids because she got involved with the families and different traditions. It was really cool.

Through this family-based activity Kim felt known and understood. In an increasingly culturally diverse society this type of activity promotes a sense of belonging, accompanied by mutual respect and understanding.

BULL SESSION

"I believe we can change the world if we start listening to one another again. Simple, honest, human conversation."

~ Margaret Wheatley

Aric, a master teacher of mathematics, shared this story from his high school years:

> My high school history teacher, Mr. Trenkler, would just randomly, while kids were working, call students up to his desk just to shoot the bull. He'd say, "Aric, come here." Then he'd sit me at his desk and ask, "How's track going?" or some other question just to start a conversation. After a while he did it so much that I finally figured out that he just wanted to get to know ya, and that kind of relationship actually worked for me. I teach math so history was not really my bag. He seemed like he was interested, it wasn't like it was a forced conversation. It can be hard to talk about yourself, but he asked me to describe myself, various things like band, sports, hunting and fishing. And he did that for all the students. He really wanted to know us and it did spark more interest in history for me.

There is no better way to know our students than through simple conversation. Some might consider this a waste of time but it was integral to Mr. Trenkler's art of teaching. It may not reflect the science of teaching, but we need both art and science to capture the hearts of our students.

WHAT TEACHERS AND STUDENTS SAY

*"Very common is the desire for a fuller knowledge of one another,
a yearning for a kind of psychological intimacy and psychological
proximity and of being fully known to each other."*

~ Abram Maslow

Students and teachers agree that knowing students well contributes to creating high levels of commitment and achievement as well as a sense of belonging for our students. Students are acutely aware of a teacher's willingness to know their students as unique individuals who live most of their lives outside of school. Students want to be known as hard-working, diligent, and successful. They also want to be known as artists, musicians, political activists, athletes, siblings, sons and daughters, and so much more.

We must become "students of our students." We learn any subject by observing, questioning, listening, and engaging. The desire to be known is one of the most powerful yearnings of the human soul. Addressing this need strengthens the student-teacher relationship and equips us with important insights to address the unique emotional and cognitive needs of our students.

The most basic level is to know each student's name. For teachers who have large classes this can be a real challenge, especially early in the year. Paula addresses this challenge by "taking my yearbook home to study it because of the new kids. I don't know them yet and I need to." Shayla, a student, related the following story about a new guidance counselor in her school. "She was like the sweetest lady in the whole world. She learned everyone's name right away! She came here and I had never even seen her before and she like, 'Oh, how are you?' And she knew my name! I was like, how did you know my name?" Irish poet Gerald Griffin once wrote, "A place in thy memory, dearest, is all that I claim; to pause and look back when thou hearest the sound of my name." Making the effort to learn the names of all our students even before we meet them sends a powerful message that we have an interest in them as unique individuals.

Kim, an elementary teacher, uses the students' names in lessons throughout the day. In math she describes word problems such as, "If

Daniel brought five candy bars to school and shared three with Eli, how many does Daniel have left for himself?" In language arts while learning about proper nouns, Kim will say, "Find the proper nouns in my sentence. Anna ran races with Grace, Clara, and Malena." Integrating student names into the lesson is a natural way for students to hear the beautiful sound of their own name.

James, a mid-school teacher, describes the importance of knowing students on a personal basis: "I guess one of the most important things is indicating that you have an interest in their outside life other than just school. To find out what their interests are, maybe if they are on a sporting team, maybe how they did last night during the game. Just a general wanting to know more about that person and finding out about their everyday life outside of school."

Phillip, a high school science teacher, suggests, "I try to find out something personal about them, about their interests, something about their family and whether I can make a connection with them that way. By making that connection they know that you really care about them as an individual and not just because they are students in the class."

Fay and Funk (1995) suggest the "one sentence intervention" (p. 21) as a means to express interest in our students. The teacher begins with the words, "I noticed…" and then says something positive, true, but unrelated to schoolwork. Through this simple intervention we affirm the student while communicating that the student is not just another number in the classroom. Fay and Funk say, "This intervention is based on the research that shows that a student's improved behavior or cooperation can be traced and linked to the personal connection he/she developed with a special adult" (Fay and Funk, 1995, p. 22).

Heavy class loads make this very challenging. Marc shared one of his greatest fears when he told me,

> The one that scares me the most, and I probably do it, is simply to not notice them, to not even see them. You get 148 students coming through your door every day and sometimes there's one or two that you literally don't see and that's scary for me. Especially for the kid who is already thinking, "I don't matter." Nobody does that

deliberately, but maybe it's because you can only spread yourself so thin. And why I think that is so scary is that you probably don't even know if you're doing it.

Most of us can solve problems we are aware of; the difficulty comes when we don't know that a problem exists. It makes me wonder about my own blind spots. What don't I notice about my students or staff members?

Denise, who works with at-risk students, shares her perspective:

> It's almost like the more a teacher cares about his or her students the more that child will want to give back to the teacher. Sometimes just the little things a teacher says, does, or notices, is all it takes to impact the students. Noticing when a child was gone and asking them how they're doing the next day, or complimenting them on a new hairstyle, hair color, or a new outfit. This is something that takes a total of thirty seconds but demonstrates one hundred fold that you care about them unconditionally.

Chris, an elementary teacher, really likes to focus on her students' families. "I love to get to know the child's family because it helps me know the child better. I'll ask questions about their families and the things they do together. Parent-teacher conferences are great opportunities to get even more information, background, and insights into each child."

Sam goes out of his way and uses any excuse to interact with students. "I find that as I go from my room to the copier, wherever I go, I talk in the halls. I am tardy to every class, just saying 'hi' to kids. They like it, and when you see them outside of school, that is really important to them and a great bridge builder. I've had other colleagues tell me, 'The weekend—that's MY time.' I enjoy it when I'm at the mall and run into students and shoot the breeze. I think it's part of the job."

Peter, a student, shares his thoughts: "One thing that I really appreciate is when teachers talk to us in the halls. Like when they pass you they say, 'Hey, how are you doing today?' They may ask you what you've been up to, how'd the game go, and stuff like that. And generally, I think for most people it gives them a sense of well, it's not going to be a bad day. Most people when they get up they are like, 'I'm tired, I want to go back to bed.' But if they come to school and are greeted by a teacher that they like or even one that they may not like, if they are treated in a positive manner you think, 'Okay, I guess it's not as bad as I thought.'" When students believe it's "not as bad as I thought," that's a start. Students with positive attitudes are equipped to learn.

Angela shared this unique insight from the perspective of a graduating senior: "I know like especially when it's your senior year they ask about our future plans. They already know about our past. Now they are curious to know where we are going to go from here when they are not with us every day anymore. I think that's really cool. It shows that it wasn't just thirteen years of schooling but it was a bond, a friendship that was built." This enduring type of relationship is one of the psychic rewards that provide meaning to our work.

The following conversation involves several high school students talking about teachers:

"I love Mrs. Krantz, and that she remembered me after all these years. She was my first grade teacher. When I was in high school, she still remembered my name and that has always made me feel good."

"Like Miss Stefanatz, I saw her at the mall this weekend. Some teachers, they'll pretend like they don't see you there. But Miss Stefanatz came right up to me and said, 'Hey, how's it going?' She started talking to me about her favorite band. And it's like we were just two adults having a chat. That was cool."

"Miss Kunkel did that to me yesterday. I was working and she came up to me and she said, 'Hey!' And she started to talk to me and stuff."

"Even when they just say, you know, 'How's it going?' That just opens up so many new doors."

"Or if they take time to ask questions during class or before class. Like when they ask you something about other things not in regards to that class but maybe something that you did that weekend. Or when they talk to you like a normal person and not as a student, like they've known you for a really long time."

"Even our elementary teachers, you see them in the hall and they still know who you are. They just remember. It makes for a better learning environment to know them and they know you. You have a connection. From there you can go almost anywhere."

There is no downside to getting to know our students well. The result is always positive, wherever and however we make that connection.

COACH ANDRIST

"I have learned that when we begin listening to each other, and when we talk about things that matter to us, the world begins to change."

~ Margaret Wheatley

Along with being known, I knew Coach Andrist quite well. He was a rock. Nothing could shake him. Today we would call him a grounded person. Coach possessed that rare quality of being a person you could always count on; he was sturdy.

Coach Andrist and I primarily spent time together through wrestling, but we also shared time hunting, fishing, playing cards, going to athletic events, and even going to movies. We could talk about anything. Coach had an eclectic and inquiring mind. He was well versed and widely experienced in a variety of topics. I was very interested in what he thought and had to say because he was interested in me.

Obviously this unique association is impossible to develop in every student-teacher relationship. But many teachers develop similar relationships with students every day. Consider the impact if every student, particularly needy students, had just one teacher who invested themselves in this depth of relationship. What a profound difference this would make in the lives of our students. Coach's personal interest contributed to developing my confidence, maturity, and resilience. Each one of us can make the same contribution to the lives of our youth. A great place to start is by getting to know each student well.

Avoid Ignoring Students

"When people are deaf, I am dumb."

~ Joseph Joubert

Max, a fifth grade teacher, describes an incident where a teacher did not know the name of one of her students at a parent-teacher conference.

> This teacher didn't know the child's name. She didn't know the kid they were talking about. Yeah, and it was an average kid, quiet kid, and because the teacher didn't know—you can imagine the flavor that parent has for our school district—unbelievably negative feelings for the school. At an elementary level you wouldn't think you would have that many students and should know them all by the end of the first quarter. But she didn't. She (the parent) talked about that incident for years, even when her daughter was in high school.

None of us want to make that mistake, but it can happen so easily if we don't make the conscious effort to know each student. Consider an "average" kid who is quiet and unassuming in a class of thirty students. This student doesn't cause any problems and is reluctant to answer questions or share in class. We have to deal regularly with higher maintenance students who command our time, and we never get around to making that personal connection with this "average kid." It could happen to any of us.

Ignoring students negatively impacts student achievement (Palmer, 1983). When we ignore or are dismissive of a student's ideas we are essentially saying, "I don't care to know you or what you may think." Students reported to me that they particularly didn't appreciate teachers who "ignore and disregard what I say," "don't value my opinions," or "don't listen to my point of view." While students are very forgiving, they understandably have little tolerance for a dismissive attitude from adults.

A WORD OF ENCOURAGEMENT

"We can change the world if we start listening to one another again."

~ Margaret Wheatley

Many teachers have class loads that make knowing each student well a daunting task. Please do not despair. All important things take time. Be patient and persistent. When we apply some of the practices offered by our fellow professionals cited above, it will simply be a matter of time before we feel confident in our relationships. The reciprocal nature of love is undeniable. When our students feel valued, they value what we are offering. The better we know each student and the more our students feel loved, the greater investment students will make in our classes.

Some students have never experienced a sense of belonging in school or had a meaningful student-teacher relationship. When you show genuine interest in a student, he or she may be understandably skeptical, rejecting your efforts to build a relationship. Human nature's desire for connection and your willingness to love will eventually win out. As Carl Rogers (1983) suggests, "If only one teacher out of one hundred dared to risk, dared to be, dared to trust, dared to understand, we would have an infusion of a living spirit into education that would, in my estimation, be priceless" (p. 131). The relationships we build with our students are priceless. I encourage you to dare to love, dare to know, dare to be known.

BECOMING A STUDENT OF OUR STUDENTS

"Teachers should know their students and students, in turn, should know their teachers."

~ G. I. Maerhoff

Knowing students well may best be described as becoming students of our students. That may sound trite, too obvious to discuss, or just common sense. But common sense is seldom common practice. We break this process down into five components that can take place independently or simultaneously. They follow the basic scientific method of noticing a phenomenon, asking questions about what one sees, listening to the answers to those questions, and then engaging in conversation to gain a more complete understanding. The fifth component is to "be there." Be at those activities that are most important to our students and through which their passion and strengths are revealed.

1. NOTICE

"The most important thing in communication is to hear what isn't being said."

~ Peter Drucker

Awareness of what is happening in the lives of our students is the first step in getting to know our students well. While simply noticing is an admittedly superficial level of understanding, it does open the door for more in-depth interactions. When we notice that a student has put more effort into class and is doing well, is struggling academically or personally, performed well in a concert, or recently became an Eagle Scout, the foundation is laid for deeper understanding and engagement. Loving teachers notice all they can as a means to understanding the unique qualities and needs of each student.

Noticing small, everyday occurrences is a meaningful way to connect with students. It can be as easy as saying, "Oh, you got your hair cut," "I like that color shirt on you," or "I've noticed you're not yourself today." When a student misses class we should express concern about getting them back on track. Noticing what extra and co-curricular activities students are involved in is also important. For many students their identity and sense of belonging is strongly tied to these activities. Art, a mid-school teacher, told me, "You see kids in the hall and you notice they may be in band or that they might be on the yearbook staff and those kinds of things. And I think that kind of connection where you can make that first step, that initial contact with them, by simply saying, 'I see you had a good game last night,' or 'you did a nice job at the concert,' or whatever it might be. And I think that's a good start." When we notice the unique characteristics of our students, they feel that we are making an effort to get to know them as a whole person, not just "another head in the classroom."

Petra, a high school student, shared a story about an art teacher whose awareness had an impact on her life.

> This happened in middle school before I had taken any art classes. The art teacher pulled me out of a class one day because she somehow got ahold of some sketches I had in my notebook. Anyway she pulled me out of the class and said she had seen some of my stuff and she gave me a drawing notepad and some drawing pencils and told me to keep them as long as I used them. It was just an odd recognition and I still have the drawing pad that is full of sketches. I don't know, just being recognized from other people that you didn't even know recognized you, was really nice.

Practice awareness. Notice anything and everything you can about your students. Study them as you would the skies through a telescope or cells under a microscope. What we learn equips us to serve in ways we might never have imagined.

2. ASK

"Curiosity is a great help to good conversation…It creates a spaciousness that is rare in other interactions. It takes time to create this space, but as we feel it growing, we speak more truthfully and the conversation moves into what's real."

~ Margaret Wheatley

Asking questions is a natural way to get to know our students while expressing genuine interest in their well-being and development. Students observed that questions from teachers come in many forms. For example, teachers might ask "questions about me—more personal—like family life, sports," "about future goals, college," or "If I'm having a bad day, ask if I'm okay or if I need to talk about it." Students similarly accented the importance of questions directed at their academic progress such as, "If I am struggling, some teachers will ask if I need or want extra help," and, "If I am falling behind, they ask what is going on and how they can help."

I don't know if this is still common practice, but when I was in grade school we often started the year by writing a short paper entitled "What I did last summer." I wonder if my teachers did this, at least in part, to learn something personal about each of us. It may have been a way to gauge our writing skills, but it may have been more. Those teachers may have been students of their students.

3. LISTEN

"Listening is a magnetic and strange thing, a creative force. The friends who listen to us are the ones we move toward. When we are listened to, it creates us, makes us unfold and expand."

~ Karl Menninger

Just as we are drawn to friends who are good listeners, students are drawn to us when we listen—really listen—to them. The most important but most neglected communication skill is listening. To listen effectively, one must listen with both the ears and the heart (Hoyle, 2002). Listening demonstrates value and respect which makes students far more likely to engage in learning and reciprocate through respectful behavior (McCaslin and Good, 1996).

Listening helps us to understand students' thought processes and develop their thinking and problem-solving skills. A good question followed by active listening encourages students to challenge and evaluate the structures on which they build their arguments. This process unfolds the latent intellect of our students. Through active listening we introduce students to themselves and the unlimited potential of the human mind. Active listening requires high levels of concentration to perceive exactly what each student is saying, feeling, and experiencing. When our student feels like they are the most important person in the world during these exchanges, we have reached the proper level.

Listening requires patience: the key element in wait time. Wait time is the pause we make between asking a question and ending the opportunity for the student to respond (Brophy, 1981). Pausing three or more seconds dramatically increases the students' use of language and logic (Rowe, 1986). Through patience we communicate our belief that students can think for themselves, and our faith in their ability to articulate a reasoned response. As Patty explained, her teachers "earn my respect when they listen to my ideas and help me with my thoughts."

Flanders (1961) found that the typical teacher talks about 66% of the time during class. Teachers of high achieving students only talk about 55% of the time, and teachers of low achieving students talk about 80% of the time. Expecting students to talk about the subject rather than passively listening to the teacher facilitates learning.

So what do teachers hear when students are willing to share? "They listen to your comments, no matter how ignorant," says student Thomas. That sums it up pretty well. Be willing to listen to everything. You will hear things that you wish you hadn't, but that goes with the territory. When students know we are willing to listen to everything, we open the door to deeper understanding and greater levels of engagement. Students like Patricia also appreciate it when "they listen to me when I am expressing a problem and they give positive feedback." Kevin knows that teachers have listened when "they know certain things about you because you told them and they remembered."

We close this segment with the following conversation between two master teachers:

"Today I had a student come to me, concerned about her ACT score," said the first. "The colleges that she wants to get into won't accept that low of a score even though she has a very strong grade point average. She was distraught. I chose to listen to her even though I wanted to get back to work. But no, no, I'll listen. Basically you kind of commiserate with them and just say, 'Well, you know, there are some other things you can do here.' She couldn't take the

ACT this time around because of the sectional basketball play-offs. If she took the retake test she would have to miss the game. Then her coach is going to be mad at her and she was concerned because he told her to just forget the season if she did that. So she was very concerned about what to do with that. She needed someone to listen to her today."

"Think about that," responded the other. "She's feeling like she's between a rock and a hard place here. You were this outlet for her, somebody who stopped and listened and at least offered a sympathetic ear. You might not be able to fix it but at least you listened to her concern."

Sometimes all we can do is listen. We may not be able to offer counsel that the student accepts or understands. Nevertheless, sensitively listening to a student's concern is an act of love which can help them through difficult times. Sensitive listening is the best way to develop an understanding for students. Carl Rogers suggests that listening "of this very special kind, is one of the most potent forces for change that I know" (Rogers, 1980, p. 116).

4. Caring Conversations

"Conversation is an opportunity to meet together as peers, not as roles. What makes us equal is that we're human beings."

~ Margaret Wheatley

Noticing, asking questions, and listening are all ways that teachers enter into caring conversations. Caring conversations make students feel, "I'm a real person and not just another faceless student." Being fully known by even one adult can make all the difference in how students see themselves, their school, and the value of learning.

Mendler's (2001) 2x10 method is particularly effective when trying to connect with hard-to-know students. The formula is simple. Spend two minutes talking with an identified student for ten successive school days. The conversation may include school topics, but it is most effective when the discussion focuses on some other interest of the student. This builds rapport and has healed many combative student-teacher relationships.

On the elementary level in particular, morning meetings are a good tool for getting to know students, for helping students to know each other, and for building a family-like classroom atmosphere. While the meeting usually includes sharing the plan for the day, it is also a great time to check in with students and discover if there are any emotional issues that need attention. Classroom meetings in which students and teachers discuss personal, behavioral, and academic issues in a non-judgmental environment also engender a sense of acceptance in the classroom (Marzano, 1992).

Kerry summarized the student perspective when he shared, "I appreciate the teachers who always ask like how's your day, and what things are going on, and what are you interested in, and like how you are doing in sports, too. Sometimes they will come to the games and try to make sporting events and stuff. It shows that they care about you. Yes—at school they are paid to be there—I'm your teacher, it's my job—but when they talk to you in the hall and talk to you outside school—they don't get paid to do that."

5. Be There

"Ninety percent of success is just showing up."

~ Anonymous

While presenting to a group of teachers from large metropolitan schools a few years ago, I asked, "How many of you have attended an extra or co-curricular school event in the past year?" Having spent most of my career in small schools, I was shocked at how few hands went up. Fewer than a dozen hands were raised, out of over 120 attendees. In smaller schools it is not unusual to have a majority, if not the entire faculty, at a game, concert, or play. Sometimes we have better attendance at school activities than we have at faculty meetings. Perhaps that's because there isn't a whole lot to do on a Friday night in small town America. But I know it is more than that. Those teachers are there to support their students and to show that they value what is important to their students. "Being there" involves spending time beyond the school day, attending events where our students showcase their talents. As Carly, a student, shared with us, "When teachers come to your plays or programs or activities, whether it is a football game or a concert outside of school, and notice your strength in that, that can be really encouraging to all students." Acknowledging student strengths, even if they do not apply directly to the classroom, is important to our students and a tangible way to demonstrate our love for them.

I encourage you to become a student of your students: make that personal connection, find out what they are passionate about and what really makes them tick. When you do, you will capture their hearts and make everything else possible.

"A LIFETIME OF LOVING SERVICE"

"The least of the work of learning is done in the classroom…"

~ Thomas Merton

One of my most influential mentors was Mr. Jerry Berseth, commonly referred to as "Mr. B." Mr. B's career of service embodied "being there" as well as "going the extra mile." He served as high school principal and activities director for over thirty years. In all that time he never missed a game, concert, play, or other activity in which his students performed. For this and many other reasons, Mr. B was loved and respected by students, staff, and the community.

Co- and extra-curricular activities are often described as "the other half of education." Mr. B was the biggest advocate for activities in Fall Creek, Wisconsin. His school of less than 300 students had outstanding programs in virtually every area. During his tenure, the Crickets won multiple state championships in a variety of sports, had a vocal and instrumental music program that was the pride of the community and which produced many professional artists, a drama program that put on every kind of performance and produced several professional performers, a robust Future Farmers of America program that produced state and national level leaders, National Honor

Society and Student Council programs that provided valuable service throughout the community, and an art program that was second to none. Under Mr. B's direction, over 90% of the student body was involved in at least one activity, with most students being involved in several. This is very impressive when you consider that only 58% of youth nationwide spend three hours or more in a productive after-school activity (Scales and Leffert, 2004). It was the norm to have linemen from the state championship football team as part of the Show Choir or as participants in the Spring Musical. Mr. B actively encouraged every student to be part of some activity because when they have a connection to the school outside of the classroom they inevitably do well in the classroom. Fall Creek regularly had the highest test scores in west-central Wisconsin as measured by state and national testing standards. The ACT scores were always above the state and national averages and 80% of his students went on to some post-secondary educational option.

Mr. B understood and promoted the connection between the classroom and school activities, but he also walked the talk by being present at every activity. In describing his commitment as an educator Mr. B wrote, "Love and other positive relationships will develop roots when we as educators realize our purpose is 24/7, when our commitment to the student has depth. There is no time clock in education." To "be there" is to go beyond the time clock, giving our time and attention to what matters most to the students.

Students are far more likely to buy into the school experience when we take a personal interest in their lives and go out of our way to get to know them well. The old saying "They don't care how much you know until they know how much you care" applies. Through a personal connection we gain insight into each student's natural gifts, which enhances our ability to educate and draw forth those gifts.

"What scholars now say—and what good teachers have always known—is that real learning does not happen until students are brought into relationship with the teacher, with each other, and with the subject. We cannot learn deeply and well until a community of learning is created in the classroom"

~ Parker J. Palmer

Chapter Two:
Vision

Why Vision Is Love and Why It Matters

"Don't ask what the world needs. Ask what makes you come alive, and go do it. Because what the world needs is people who have come alive."

~ Howard Thurman

Vision involves seeing through the eyes of love, seeing the best in our students to help them see the best in themselves. Vision sees beyond the faults and failings that are part of the human condition, and embraces the greatness, the genius that each student possesses. We all have faults and failings. We also possess gifts—incredible gifts that we have an obligation to develop and share for our own needs as well as to contribute to the greater good. Every student we serve provides evidence, sometimes well hidden, of exceptional talents which will help them come alive and claim their place in the world. We are, in a sense, introducing students to themselves when we help them discover their gifts.

Crafting a vision of worth and potential in the mind of a student is like painting a beautiful landscape while leaving the intricate details to the student's ample imagination. Chinese folklore depicts the teacher as "the hand pointing toward the moon." What a wonderful way of describing the practice of providing a vision for the student, expressing their limitless potential while understanding it is the student's responsibility to determine their own path. Providing a vision involves both the science and art of teaching. Developing an awareness of student strengths requires the discernment of a scientist. Communicating those strengths in a convincing fashion requires artistry to develop symbols of communication that fire the imagination of the student.

The specific vision itself is less important than the sense of purpose and accomplishment it compels. Consider the loss for mankind if Michelangelo, Mozart, Thomas Aquinas, or Galileo had not developed or shared their talents. The world for each of us would be diminished. In our classrooms today there are students who possess the seeds of equal or greater contribution than all of these historical icons. The world needs every student to realize their potential in order to complete the tapestry of the human experience. Without loving adults who can communicate a compelling vision we will continue to experience the greatest of human tragedies—lives unfulfilled. When every young man and woman recognizes the greatness and beauty they carry within themselves, all of mankind will experience the destiny for which we are intended; only then will the fullness of the human experience be realized. When we see the best in our students and vividly communicate a compelling vision of their worth and potential, we help them come alive. We are "the hand pointing toward the moon."

MY DAD—A PERSONAL INTERLUDE

"Love can only exist in freedom. The true lover seeks the good of his beloved which requires especially the liberation of the beloved from the lover."

~ Anthony de Mello

I was the youngest of six brothers, all outstanding athletes, with most excelling in basketball. Dad put up a basketball hoop at the end of the driveway, and it was one of the busiest places around our house. We played very physical, competitive games at that hoop. We played for hours with friends and neighbors who dropped by. If it was just us Nolan boys, we seldom played a game that didn't end in a fight, but that's another story.

I enjoyed basketball and knew the family expectation that we would all play basketball in high school. When I started wrestling in junior high and quit basketball, it caused a rift between my father and me. The only wrestling he had ever experienced was the television theatrics that masqueraded as wrestling. Today it is big money and is commonly known as the WWF. Back then it was low grade melodrama with overweight, over-the-hill, wannabe athletes.

Any parent takes great joy in watching their son or daughter perform in a play, concert, or athletic event. This was true for Lisa and I as it was for my mother and father who never missed a game or performance. Dad was disappointed when I chose to wrestle but he never insisted that I play basketball. He advised: "No matter what you do, be the best." That's all he wanted. Dad's vision was that each of us would, no matter what we chose to pursue, become the best we could be. Dad gave me the freedom to be myself rather than a carbon copy of my five older brothers. The following stories illustrate how teachers offered a vision that changed how students viewed themselves and their place in the world.

A VISIONARY COACH

"Education is about healing and wholeness. It is about empowerment, liberation, transcendence and renewing the vitality of life. It is about finding and claiming ourselves and our place in the world."

~ Parker J. Palmer

Bill, a high school student, shared the unexpected vision offered by his cross-country running coach. Bill was a below-average athlete who persisted in competing in the grueling sport of cross-country running despite experiencing little success. Coach Ryan's vision helped him see the sport, as well as his transcendent role on the team, in its proper perspective. Coach Ryan once said to Bill, "You know, you are one of the worst runners on the team; you are really slow;

and you finish last in almost every meet. But I have to admit you add something to the team and I think you are a really good leader." When asked how Coach's comments influenced him, Bill replied, "When Coach Ryan would say things like that, the running becomes less important and you focus on what you are good at. I never really thought of myself as, 'Oh, maybe I'm a team leader,' it was always, 'Oh, I'm really bad at running.' But then it changed my focus and I concentrated more on the other things. You gain a new confidence when somebody tells you something like that."

What a beautiful example of the wisdom, beauty, and blessings of a loving teacher. Coach Ryan exercised wisdom in his honesty; he didn't sugarcoat the fact that Bill wasn't much of a runner. Covering that up would have been disingenuous, making Coach Ryan's more salient point less credible. If Coach Ryan had patronizingly told Bill, "You could be a state champion," or some other fairy tale, he would likely have damaged their relationship. The beauty is that Coach Ryan saw something in Bill—leadership, which the teenager had not seen in himself. He then took the initiative to communicate that vision so clearly that Bill began to see it too. Through this blessing Bill was enabled to focus on the real purpose of athletics—developing individual character—by seeing himself as a burgeoning young leader regardless of his competitive accomplishments. It is not often that a coach identifies the least effective performer on the team as a team leader. Coach Ryan's insight made all the difference in how Bill defined himself and his place in the world.

The next two stories involve master teachers whose career choices were very much influenced by teachers that they respected. In both cases a career as an educator was not something they had considered prior to the intervention by their mentors. Our profession is lucky to have both of these young men in the trenches with us.

The Power of a Single Conversation

"Leaders are dealers in hope."

~ Napoleon

Matt had it all planned: after high school he was going on to the local college, then medical school, followed by a successful career as a physician. That sounds like a wonderful story, and it may very well have happened that way had it not been for a ten-minute conversation Matt had with his high school science teacher. It was late in the second semester of his senior year when Mr. Patrick invited Matt into his office. During their conversation Mr. Patrick shared a vision with Matt in which he identified Matt's attributes, reinforcing his sense of self-worth, and then described how those attributes would make Matt an outstanding teacher. Mr. Patrick closed by saying, "We need more people like you in our profession." When Matt shared this experience with me, I imagined Uncle Sam in his red, white, and blue top hat pointing his finger and saying, "I want you!" It is a great feeling to be wanted. As a result of that conversation, Matt changed his plans, pursued a teaching career, and developed into an outstanding educator. Mr. Patrick was right; we can never have too many good people in our profession.

"I think about how pivotal that moment was because that affected my whole life," says Matt. "I was going to go to a different school and I changed schools. As it turned out that's how I met my wife. I did a lot of things based on that one conversation. I never really entertained that idea previously. But I have never regretted my decision to become a teacher. Mr. Patrick moved to Arizona. He just passed away, but I wrote him a note every year for 20 years saying, 'Thanks a lot. I still love what I'm doing. I couldn't think of any other career that I'd rather have.' But obviously he didn't need to do that, take the time to sit down and talk to me like that."

But he did take the time, which resulted in a fulfilling life and career of meaningful contributions for Matt. Don't be shy about communicating to students their worth and potential, and how they might best put them to use. They may be only vaguely aware, if not oblivious, to the potential for greatness that is their birthright.

We never know how one conversation might positively influence a student's life. In this case it produced a very fine teacher who is a credit to our profession.

The Lost Soul

"What you see in others has more to do with who you are than who the other people are."

~ Epictetus

Marty is a master science teacher who is universally respected by his students and peers. He has had a long and distinguished career, including being selected numerous times by his students as their most influential teacher. Marty has also worked as a wildlife biologist and is sought after as a consultant to companies developing new biology texts. One might assume that with such an impressive résumé Marty always knew what his path in life would be, but this was not the case. Like Matt it was the vision of a teacher that encouraged Marty's career choice.

> Looking back at my own life, it was my high school biology teacher (Mr. Barron) who was inspirational to me in choosing my career, in that he let me know that I could do it. He told me I had a good aptitude for remembering the names and spellings of scientific terms. I guess he just let me know that I had a gift for this area. As a senior in high school I didn't have a clue where I was going to end up. I was always filled with self-doubt when I was in high school, and I didn't have a clue as to which direction I was headed. But Mr. Barron let me know that this was something that I could do well. I had a difficult time with my father and I guess I was searching for a role model type person and he just kind of became that for me. He was a real positive influence on me. He definitely pointed me down this road.

Mr. Barron planted a seed in Marty which provided a purpose, a vision for his life. This vision has enriched Marty's life as well as the thousands of students that Marty has taught and mentored over his career.

The Arkansas Travelers

"Treat a man as he appears to be, and you make him worse. But treat a man as if he were what he potentially could be, and you make him what he should be."

~ Johann Wolfgang von Goethe

Cheryl and Joanna concluded that for their at-risk students to flourish they needed to get them out of their comfort zones, to be challenged in a fashion that went beyond the normal curriculum.

Cheryl describes their experience, "Joanna and I have been doing a lot of teaming with at-risk students. A couple of years ago we had a group that was absolutely incorrigible, so we decided that we needed to cut a bit of the curriculum and find a way to get these kids involved in school and teach them something about respect for one another, themselves, and the world. We needed these students to see themselves differently. Belief and faith came into play in a big way when we helped these fifteen students raise enough money to get on a bus and ride down to the state of Arkansas for a weekend. I mean there was no end to the people who said to us, 'Are you nuts?!' These were kids who had never been away from home and who came from all kinds of situations. Our goal was to provide them with a different perspective on life, to let that experience take root with them, and it became an incredible bonding experience with those kids as well as a great teaching and learning experience for us."

Joanna added, "We went to work at the Heifer Ranch in Arkansas, but we also did a lot of team-building activities. The Heifer Ranch is an educational farm in rural Arkansas committed to ending hunger and poverty in the world. We wanted our students to see and be part of a movement like that, you know, something bigger than themselves."

Cheryl explained, "Part of the experience was staying in a local garage. I mean sleeping all night on a cement floor as a forty-year-old next to a seventeen-year-old boy, I'm thinking, 'This is just too uncomfortable.' And then the whole experience of waking up with them saying, 'you really snore.' What do you talk about to the girl who has never left her dysfunctional family and has never left town and she cries all night because she is lonesome? And so-and-so misses his mom because she just got out of jail today and he regrets being here because he thinks he needs to be there for her. Being in that environment and helping those students through those issues, I mean that was just an amazing experience."

Another colleague added, "As someone who has had those same kids on both sides, I had them as freshmen and now they are juniors. Those kids are forever changed because of that experience and for the better."

Cheryl and Joanna identified a need, developed a vision of how to address that need, and gave their students the chance to grow and perform beyond even their own expectations. Cheryl and Joanna saw more in their students than the students saw in themselves. I've traveled a lot with students; I can well imagine the anxiety Cheryl and Joanna must have dealt with concerning this excursion. Nevertheless, they were willing to make the effort and trust that this experience would be a leap of faith worth taking. This is another example where students, when seen through the eyes of love, exceed expectations. I applaud Cheryl and Joanna for their insight, imagination, and courage in creating such a wonderful opportunity for their students.

Tim—Never, Never, Never Give Up

"Love them, especially when they least deserve to be loved."

~ Kate Samperi

Gary, a high school wrestling coach, offers the following story illustrating the power of a vision as it applied to Tim, a young man who, for a time, lacked any real direction or purpose in his life. Tim had a checkered background when he came out of junior high. Despite being a bright kid, he never really applied himself so his academic performance was a mixed bag. Several junior high teachers had given up on Tim; one commented that "he was never going to amount to anything and was not worthy of my time."

Despite a history of poor choices, Tim had a heart of gold. Like other kids his age he was easily seduced into doing things that were not in his best interest. Fundamentally, Tim lacked a positive vision for his life; however, Tim was a gifted wrestler, so Gary and a few other teachers committed to making Tim their personal project for the next four years. They hoped to use Tim's interest in wrestling as a vehicle to provide direction and purpose—to help him experience some success and transfer that to other aspects of his life. Gary and the others let Tim know that they would never give up on him. In his freshman year Tim became academically ineligible at the semester. This was not a big surprise, as Tim had not paid the price academically in mid-school to prepare for the challenges of high school work. The counselor provided the academic help he needed and Tim took advantage of it. Tim continued to practice with the team through the rest of the season although he could no longer compete.

During his sophomore year Tim turned the corner academically and had a great year on the mat. With about a month left in the season, Tim violated the school's athletic code policy by not leaving a party where alcohol was present. Even though Tim had not been drinking, he was ineligible to compete for the remainder of the season. But Tim didn't make any excuses for his infraction. He began to see the bigger picture: realizing that he had not only denied himself an opportunity to wrestle at the state tournament, but had also let down his teammates. This realization would not have been a consideration for Tim a year earlier. For the remainder of the year Tim continued to practice with the team, helping his teammates get better.

In his junior and senior years Tim made the honor roll in every grading period. He also became one of his school's few two-time state wrestling champions. Tim had developed into an effective leader and was one of the driving forces in bringing home his school's first team trophy from the state tournament. In four years Tim had experienced a total transformation; he was not the same kid who had entered high school. The catalyst for change was the vision that a small group of loving adults shared with Tim, along with a commitment to never give up on him. This team of educators saw the best in Tim before he could see it in himself. Tim chose to embrace that vision and work hard to bring it to fruition.

WHAT TEACHERS AND STUDENTS SAY

"What lies behind us and what lies before us are small matters compared to what lies within us."

~ Ralph Waldo Emerson

As the stories above illustrate, vision involves seeing the best in our students when they cannot see it in themselves. The intent is that they will see, and expect more of themselves. Quite often the vision is not directly tied to what we are teaching but is part of the more complete development of the whole child. The subjects we are teaching is simply the vehicle through which larger life lessons are taught. The following insights from teachers and students exemplify the positive influence that vision has on our students.

Simone, a high school student, alluded to the power of teaching life lessons through a vision when she stated, "I don't think people remember which teacher taught them how to add 2 + 2 or where to place a comma. They remember other nice things about them like this teacher taught me about self-confidence, or that teacher helped me to realize my capabilities, or another teacher helped me find my goal. That's what we truly remember and value."

Marty, a science teacher, describes his method for instilling a positive vision in students this way: "One thing I try to do is get them to realize that, okay, maybe you are not a great chemistry student and maybe this isn't so easy for you, but to let them know that there is something else for them. They may be good in English or good at memorization or any number of things. They can come down on themselves if they don't do particularly well in a certain subject area, but I try to get across the idea that everybody has a talent, what you have to do is find it." Indeed, helping students to discover their strengths is one of the great joys of teaching and a hallmark of master teachers.

Many students have a fragile self-concept, making them susceptible to getting knocked out of the saddle easily. Affirmations from teachers help boost students' self-esteem while providing a sense of well-being and belonging. Confident students take greater risks and are less likely to become frustrated (Davis and Rimm, 1989). Being reminded of one's worth and potential regularly is an essential ingredient in developing a healthy self-concept. It is one of the most fruitful ways to exhibit our love for students.

Jamie describes how she continually tracks and affirms each student:

> I schedule regular one-to-one meetings with each student. These don't have to be long meetings; five minutes will typically suffice. I schedule these times when the other students are involved with independent practice. During this time I intentionally reinforce for each student the strengths I see in them. Then I ask them what they see in themselves and how that might apply to what we are currently working on. I also try to tie what we are doing in class to their future to keep them thinking about the long haul. I am always amazed at the wonderful attributes that students miss about themselves and how this limits what they see in their future. All I really want to do is get my students to recognize their strengths and realize how many

doors those strengths can open if they will apply them. For me the structure of scheduling these check-ins is really important. If I don't schedule them, they won't happen.

Every student, even those who struggle mightily, has experienced some level of success. A regular reminder of this fact can help students build a lasting positive self-image. Too often kids have learned to focus on their weaknesses and setbacks rather than their strengths and victories. A regular part of the educational experience should be recognizing and building on one's strengths.

Teaching students two skills—affirmations and visualization—can help them sustain a vision even after they have moved beyond our influence. These practices promote refining, rehearsing, and internalizing one's vision. Peter, a social studies teacher and downhill ski coach, uses visualization with his student-athletes the day before taking a major test.

> The main thing I am looking for is that they approach each test with a relaxed confidence. It is amazing how much this has helped my students since I started doing this five or six years ago. I generally play some soft music, letting them relax for a few minutes. Then I ask some questions that are on the test asking the students to confidently, in a relaxed state, answer the questions in their mind. Like all visualizations I ask them to see themselves responding in vivid detail. What are you writing with? What is the weather like outside? If there are distractions, how are they coping, and so on? The results have been very positive and it is really neat to have students come back from college and tell me how they follow this same routine for their tests in college.

Peter has not only offered a vision of success, he has also provided a valuable tool that can be generalized to other parts of his students' lives. Influential historical figures including Albert Einstein and Napoleon Bonaparte have suggested that imagination is more important than reality. Reality consists of what is; imagination is the dwelling place of all that is possible. Everything that mankind creates starts as an idea; it starts with imagination. Visualization is a common practice for many high achievers. The great golf champion, Jack Nicklaus, never took a golf shot without first imagining the shot from start to finish: visualizing his swing, the intended flight of the ball, and the ball landing in perfect position. Many highly successful athletes, performers, and public speakers visualize executing a flawless performance before ever stepping into their arena. Visualization is like watching previews of life's coming attractions. Teaching this skill is a way to empower students to create and enhance their own vision throughout their lifetime.

We engage in self-talk during virtually all of our waking hours. Through self-talk we program our mind and attitude toward life. We can choose to program a self-concept that is healthy and positive or discouraging and negative. Research suggests that as much as 80% of self-talk is negative. Teaching students to program their minds with affirmations that are positive, personal, and present tense equips them to develop and enrich their own vision of the life they intend to live. Formally teaching the affirmation process is probably not in many curriculums throughout the country, but it should be. Affirmations teach students to love themselves by affirming their worth and potential. Affirmations also help students to fall in love with their futures, and avow that they are masters of their own destinies.

COACH ANDRIST

"The great danger for most of us is not that our aim is too high and we miss it, but that it is too low and we reach it."

~ Michelangelo

Most people's vision of a wrestler includes a fire plug build with bulging biceps, well defined musculature, a broad chest, a neck that is wider than the head, and the ability to do one-armed pull-ups. Well, not every wrestler is built that way. I was skinny as a rail and uncommonly weak. I wrestled at 155 pounds as a senior in high school and could not bench press my own weight.

The vision of becoming a state champion that Coach Andrist painted in my mind wasn't a fallacy based on overpowering strength. That would have been a fairy tale, not a vision. The vision was based on abilities I did possess or could realistically develop. What I lacked in strength I had to make up for in technique, tactics, tenacity, and conditioning. These were the directions written on Coach Andrist's hand as he pointed toward the moon.

The vision Coach Andrist had for me transcended individual accomplishment. It involved helping my teammates to improve, sharing my knowledge with young aspiring wrestlers, developing an *esprit de corps* on our team, making our school a better place, being a good son, and contributing to the community. Wrestling was the vehicle through which I could further my own cause as well as enrich the lives of others. This was the larger, more significant part of Coach Andrist's vision for me, that endures to this day.

AVOID HARSH JUDGMENT

"The more you judge, the less you love."

~ Unknown

Visioning sees the best in our students; harsh judgment focuses on faults. Vision concentrates on assets; judgment highlights short-comings. I once heard a coach vehemently yell to a student-athlete during a competition, "You'll never amount to anything." I was deeply saddened for the student as well as the coach. The student-athlete was competing with a significant health impediment and was doing the best he could under the circumstances. Each of us has probably had occasion to see a student as a glass perpetually half empty, but this type of judgment may be more indicative of our own shortcomings than a statement of fact about our students. Perhaps harsh judgment is frustration born out of our inability to successfully influence our students, or simply reflects our need to judge. Seldom is it an accurate reflection of who our students truly are.

We are all in the "process of becoming" that Maslow described (1962, 1971). The nature of "becoming"—fulfilling our true potential—often requires that we first fall short. The job description of every kid includes screwing up occasionally. Holding students accountable for their actions is the right thing to do and an act of love. Holding grudges, not allowing second and third chances, or giving up on kids, conflicts with the human tendency toward self-actualization while confirming our own status as curmudgeons. Affirming a student's inherent capacity for growth results in increased academic effort, greater academic risk taking, a more positive attitude about school, greater personal accountability, increased self-esteem, and confidence (Madden, 1997). We have a tendency to think about students in an "I'll believe it when I see it" fashion. I encourage you to switch your attitude to "when I believe it, I'll see it." Seeing the best brings out the best in our students.

When harboring doubts about a student I try to remember what it was like being a kid. Memories of my own shortcomings, some painful, remind me of how difficult it can be to find our place in the world. I am reminded of my own failings and how lucky I was to have mentors who set me on the right path, providing me a vision of a better self, better choices, and a better future. I am thankful for the teachers who furnished me with a compelling vision and chose not to judge me too harshly. In dealing with students whose actions may disappoint, we should avoid despair or manipulation. Be an artist. Paint beautiful visions in the mind of every student.

Gayle, a high school science teacher, offers this succinct illustration of what not to do:

> I have a story about an English teacher when I was in seventh grade. I remember it very specifically. It was the very first day of class and I had a brother two years older than me who had gotten into quite a bit of trouble. I walked into her class and she put us in alphabetical order. She said my name and asked if so-and-so was my brother. When I answered "yes" she said, "Well, I'm sure you are just like he is and so we won't even waste our time on you."

You can imagine the impact this had on Gayle. Making such a statement demonstrates a complete lack of belief or faith and, in this case, willingness to explore the unique gifts that Gayle possessed. Gayle has developed into a great teacher. The lesson for us seems clear: always be aware of the distinctive value, beauty, and potential of each student. We have all failed; we have all succeeded. Focus on success and leave judgment to someone else.

A Word of Encouragement

"You must give birth to your images. They are the future waiting to be born. Fear not the strangeness you feel. The future must enter you long before it happens. Just wait for the birth, for the hour of new clarity."

~ Rainer Maria Rike

Visioning plants a positive image in the mind of a student and gives them the freedom to cultivate and nurture that image to fruition. It is not a high powered sales pitch of what we want a particular student to become. It is an accurate and credible description of each student's gifts combined with suggestions of where those gifts may lead.

You may never know the impact you had when you shared a vision with a student. Choose to share the vision anyway. It may take years for the student to accept and realize the vision. Indeed, it may never happen, or it may develop in an unexpected fashion. By sharing what we see in our students they will develop a heightened sense of self, equipping them to advance more confidently in the direction of their dreams. There is no downside here. If nothing else, you have supplied this student with a coat of armor to shield them from the negative messages about themselves which they will inevitably encounter on their walk to adult maturity. Students get so much programming about how or why they don't measure up. Through advertisements they are told that they are too fat, their teeth aren't white and shiny enough, they don't drive the right car, they don't wear the right clothes, or they don't listen to the right music.

Students need to hear the good news about themselves from loving adults who see a bigger picture and a brighter future.

Be not afraid. Too often we hold back, we are tentative about sharing our feelings and insights about the students we love and serve, worrying too much about how our perceptions will be received. "Will this sound corny?" Who cares if you sound corny? Share your vision with love and let the student choose to accept, reject, or modify your gift.

Persist. Sometimes a single conversation is enough to inspire a student. For others it takes more time, more conversations, or more painting. Sometimes the most beautiful portrait takes time to develop. Never tire; never despair. Paint the portrait and leave the details to the student. They are capable. Simply be the hand pointing toward the moon.

"Love is a canvas furnished by Nature and embroidered
by imagination."

~ Voltaire

Chapter Three:
Acts of Kindness

WHY ACTS OF KINDNESS ARE LOVE AND WHY THEY MATTER

"Love is kind."

~ Paul the Apostle

Kindness is the most common, visible, and palpable manifestation of love. Loving kindness is recognized in most religious and philosophical traditions as a pillar of the human ideal. The Apostle Paul begins his masterful description of love with the words, "Love is patient, love is kind." Acts of kindness in Casper, New York, or Topeka would be recognized as acts of kindness in Tokyo, Paris, or Bogota. Kindness is a universal language that all recognize, even if words are never spoken. This also makes kindness one of the most potent expressions of love.

The words used to describe kindness may be different—compassion, benevolence, charity, generosity—but the influence is the same. Acts of kindness put us at ease, drive out fear, and bring peace to our lives. Kindness communicates, "I wish you well," "I am here for you," or "Let me share your burden." Kind behavior often subordinates our own interests for the interests of others. Kindness is living for others in the most practical, observable, and discernible sense.

Opportunities to show kindness are infinitely available. A smile, holding a door, giving up a seat, or listening are simple to do, cost us nothing, and can make someone's day or even change their entire outlook. While we sometimes focus on more notable acts of kindness, such as a large monetary donation for a worthy cause, it is the small acts of kindness in the classroom that students notice, appreciate, and emulate. One small act of kindness often ripples out to touch lives that we cannot imagine. In this sense acts of kindness are miraculous because they are so simple to do but can have such significant consequences. Bill, a student, tells us why he appreciates even the smallest acts of kindness. "It gives you a new outlook on the day. Like, if you were in a bad mood, one teacher with a warm smile and kind greeting can make a difference."

Jamie shared both the impact that loving kindness has on her and how she intends to respond. "I feel like I'm a real person and not just another faceless student. It makes me feel special and makes me want to carry the kindness on to others."

Peter described how he expresses his appreciation for his teacher's kindness: "I want to be in class and get a good grade to show the teacher they are appreciated." Loving kindness brings out the best in our students academically, socially, and emotionally.

As real models for our students, acts of loving kindness may be the most important lessons we teach. While we want to develop top mathematicians, great writers, and inquisitive scientific minds, if these students don't also develop the habit of kindness we may end up developing unethical accountants, manipulative propagandists, or unscrupulous politicians. Our unwritten curriculum—how we live before our students—must always include kindness toward ourselves and others.

The science of kindness is tied to our physiology and is reflective of love in general; that is, acts of kindness provide benefits for both the giver and the receiver. When we offer an act of kindness our body releases endorphins, morphine-like chemicals that make us feel good. This is similar to what is known as the "runner's high." Acts of kindness also cause the release of Substance P, a neurotransmitter that blocks pain. These two powerful physiological processes are the tangible manifestations of kindness, suggesting that there is a scientific basis for the maxim, "It is better to give than to receive." Studies also show that when we are recipients of kindness we experience the same physiological and psychological benefit. Even if we only witness an act of kindness the same physiological action takes place. With these substances flowing through our body we are more relaxed, joyful, optimistic, energized, and creative (Weinhold, 2007).

Let's apply this to a classroom setting. Mrs. Hathaway takes the time to comfort Jamie, a student who fell down at recess and hurt herself. It's not serious and doesn't require a call to the school nurse. Every student witnesses the kindness of Mrs. Hathaway as she helps Jamie get back on track. The physiological reactions just described are happening in every student in the room. Mrs. Hathaway, Jamie, and all of her classmates, are experiencing a natural high due to Mrs. Hathaway's kindness. Every child is more relaxed, joyful, optimistic, energized, and creative. They are ready to learn. Kindness benefits everyone and there is no downside.

The Envelope

"One sensitive teacher can nurture a lifetime love of learning. Many of us are fortunate to have had such teachers—even though no one ever scientifically measured their impact."

~ Ardit Cole

The lesson was completed and there were a few minutes of free time while the teacher took care of some unfinished business before the bell rang. While Mr. Smith worked at his computer, the students chatted about an expected class trip. Jim mentioned that he was not going to be able to go because he did not have the money. The bell rang and the students went to lunch.

Mr. Smith approached Samuel and gave him an envelope, asking that he give it to Jim anonymously. As Samuel explained,

> The envelope was sealed up and when I gave Jim the envelope and he opened it, it was like an odd amount of money, like he just sort of emptied his wallet. That teacher had expenses and tough times and just the fact that he

cared about Jim and something outside of school. That was surprising to me. Mr. Smith might not have always been a favorite, and Jim wasn't necessarily his favorite kid, but it just showed that he cared about him.

When I asked Samuel how being the intermediary in this act of kindness impacted him, he responded,

> I just saw Mr. Smith in a different way. I'll admit I wasn't always the nicest to Mr. Smith and things that were said about him I probably laughed at. But I just started to think of him as a person instead of a big, tough, uncaring individual with no feelings. Instead of just shutting off his class and saying it was stupid, I became more involved and I gave his class a second chance. I began to pay attention to what he had to say.

Mr. Smith expected that Jim would go on the class trip as a result of his kindness, but he probably never suspected the unintended consequence of his kindness: the effect it had on Samuel.

Acts of kindness have a positive impact on everyone involved. This example was truly a win-win-win situation. I do not have hard data on how Jim and Mr. Smith were affected by this act, but we know that the passive participant was deeply affected, even though the act was not directed at him. Samuel saw Mr. Smith "in a different way." It seems that he had not respected him before, but now he "started to think of him as a person." I find that statement interesting. Of course Mr. Smith was a person, but until Samuel witnessed Mr. Smith in a higher state of being, as a kind and generous individual, he did not see him as a person. Samuel's entire perspective changed. He began to "give his class a second chance" and "to pay attention to what he had to say," not because he was naturally interested in the class, nor because Mr. Smith's approach and pedagogical practices had radically changed, but because he witnessed an unanticipated act of kindness. Mr. Smith unwittingly captured Samuel's heart, which was the key to opening his mind. Never underestimate the power of kindness.

"You Look Like Hell"

"Kindness also means coming to the rescue of others when they need help, if it is in our power to supply it."

~ Lawrence G. Lovasik

On a cold January morning, Jimmy walked into Mr. Nelson's class looking pretty rough. Concerned about Jimmy's well-being, Mr. Nelson pulled Jimmy aside and said, "Jimmy, are you okay? You look like hell."

Jimmy responded with his typical smile and a half-hearted laugh, but his story warranted concern. On an evening where the temperature had settled well below zero, Jimmy had spent the night sleeping in a car. Mr. Nelson asked Jimmy to come to his office over the noon hour to discuss his situation. Over lunch Jimmy shared his story.

Jimmy's mother and father had separated years earlier and he had been living with his father and younger brother in Arizona. Jimmy's dad lost interest in being a father and the boys were left to fend for themselves. A friend and his family were moving to Wyoming. With the consent of his father, Jimmy moved with the friend's family in the summer prior to his senior year. In order to make a clean break and take full responsibility for his life, Jimmy sold his car, hired a lawyer, and filed for emancipation. The seventeen-year-old was granted legal emancipation and was now on his own. Over time, relationships became strained between Jimmy and his friend's family. Things had come to a head the night before, so Jimmy had packed up his few possessions, left the house, and spent a frigid night in an unlocked car. After the discussion with his teacher, Jimmy agreed to stay with the Nelson family for a few nights until he could get a place to stay.

After a few days it became apparent that Jimmy didn't have many options. Mr. Nelson and his wife discussed it. They moved their three children into one bedroom and made plans for Jimmy to stay with them at least through graduation in June. The Nelson children—aged one, three, and five—now had a big brother who joked with them, played with them, and "tortured" them in a fun, loving way. It seemed like Jimmy had always been a part of the family. The eight months that Jimmy lived with the Nelsons was a blessing for everyone: one of those unexpected graces that flow from kindness. There were moments of tension to be sure, but they were few and easily rectified. Jimmy graduated from high school, successfully started his own business, and eventually married and started a family of his own. Mr. Nelson's awareness, concern, and kindness were fully returned in a life-long friendship with a wonderful young man who just needed a place to live and a family that loved him.

"HERE'S TO GRANDMA"

"Concern should drive us into action and not into a depression."

~ Karen Horney

Andrew, a teacher, shared this story from his high school years.

My grandma passed away when I was a senior in high school. One thing sticks out in my mind, I don't even remember what classes I had with this particular teacher, I don't remember anything other than she was so kind to me. I was sitting in art class and she bought me a can of Coke, handed it to me and said, "Oh here, honey." And we hoisted one to Grandma. I said, "Well, thanks for the can of Coke," and she left. But she was the only teacher who acknowledged what I was dealing with. I was very close to my grandma. It was a small school—we just knew everything and everybody—and yet she was the only teacher that said she was sorry to hear about that. I was gone for several days. When we returned she caught me in the hall and said, "I'll make your family a hot dish." She brought it over that evening. I can still remember how appreciative my mother was. It was a hard time for us all. I just thought that was really nice of her. Her acts of kindness have always stuck in my mind.

Random acts of kindness do stick with us, make us better people, and spur us to pass the kindness on to others. We may not remember everything our teachers taught us, but we will always remember how we were treated. Acts of kindness teach valuable lessons.

Small Is Good

"Few of us can do great things, but all of us can do small things with great love."

~ Mother Teresa

Students appreciate the little kindnesses that we offer each day and these small, consistent acts create an ideal atmosphere for learning. Kind words have a profound impact on how students see themselves and the value of their educational experience. We do not have to open our wallets or take students into our homes to show kindness. Most acts of kindness cost us nothing and pay dividends far beyond what we imagine. The following comments come from a student whose insights reflect those of his peers.

> I think generally for me it's a bunch of small things, especially from a certain teacher I have in mind, just saying, "Well, that's a good point," or when you turn in a journal there's a comment like, "That's a really good idea." Just saying something, it doesn't even have to be a real compliment, but saying it in a complimentary way. You have something from them that shows that they really were paying attention and that they value what you are trying to do or what you are saying. In a math class when you happen to say the right number at the right time and they say, "Oh, good job!" If you get enough "good jobs," it's really all you need. Getting a good grade from them really doesn't mean as much.

LOST AND FOUND

"Kindness is loving people more than they deserve."

~ Joseph Joubert

The influence of an act of kindness can last for a long time. This story comes from Gabriella, a high school senior, who was moved by what she viewed as an uncommon act of kindness by her kindergarten teacher. Most of us would naturally do what Ms. Fields did, but nevertheless, thirteen years later Gabriella fondly remembered this act of kindness.

> When I was in kindergarten I just decided one day that I wasn't going to walk home with the person I was supposed to walk home with. I was going to walk home with a different friend of the family to her house. I didn't tell anybody so the cops were called because nobody knew where I was. I was this little kindergartner and my teacher, Ms. Fields, knew the friends of the family. They were out themselves walking around looking for me, calling friends, asking people if they had seen me at all. Ms. Fields found me and walked me back to where I was supposed to be. She didn't even yell at me. She gave me a hug and told me, "Do you know how mad your mom is going to be with you?" Then when my dad came, she just sat there and talked to my dad. She made everything seem alright. My dad didn't even tell my mom that night when she got home from work. She had to hear it the next day. When a teacher actually goes out of their way to help, I think that's so great. She went out and looked for me and that wasn't even her job, you know, that's the policeman's job. She actually cared about me. Ms. Fields still remembers me and it's a joke now. "Here's that little girl that ran away."

Kindness has a way of turning bad situations into fond memories. Ms. Fields probably had plans after school, but her loving kindness urged her to actively take part in the search for Gabriella. "Deep active caring—what I mean when I speak of kindness—involves a willingness to sacrifice one's own priorities and preferences in order to satisfy the needs of one's relating partners" (Rubin, 1983, p. 99). Ms. Fields certainly demonstrated deep active caring for Gabriella.

UNCONDITIONAL

"Love is patient."

~ Paul the Apostle

Brody, a fourth grader, was identified as oppositional-defiant, obsessive-compulsive, and a list of other behaviors that made him a real challenge for Mr. Groselek. This particular day was a rough one for Brody, capped off by his refusal to go to the bus loading area because he didn't want to do his math homework. Brody flopped on the floor and crawled under Mr. Groselek's desk. Despite the teacher's attempts to entice Brody from under the desk, he refused to come out. Mrs. Helms, the principal, was called to the classroom. Brody was given the choice to either come to the office independently or with assistance. Brody chose the latter. Mr. Groselek is a good-sized man and a former All-American football player, so assisting Brody to the office was well within his native abilities. After carrying Brody to the office Mr. Groselek carefully put him into a chair and said, "Have a good night, Brody. I'll see you in the morning." Despite the fact that Brody had been making inappropriate choices all day long, he received the same friendly farewell that every other fourth grader had received that afternoon from Mr. Groselek.

We cannot know what impact this act of kindness had on Brody. Perhaps Brody's developmental level inhibited his ability to recognize kindness. But we know that Mr. Groselek responded with the kindness that Brody needed in a situation where frustration could easily have been expected.

THANKS FOR THE MEMORIES

"Give and it will be given to you…for the measure you give will be the measure you get back."

~ Luke the Evangelist

Mrs. Palmer was a kindergarten teacher in the same Midwestern town for over thirty-five years. For all of those thirty-five years she kept a piece of artwork from each of her students. When those students graduated twelve years later she would return that piece of art work nicely wrapped in decorated envelopes. This is just one reason why Mrs. Palmer was loved by her students, colleagues, and community. She embodied loving kindness, which is what she received from the students and community she served.

Each year, even after she retired, Mrs. Palmer was invited to the high school prom to spend the evening with the students she had taught years before. She was invited to nearly every graduation party, and she made it a point to attend every one of them. While Mrs. Palmer embodied many loving traits, it was her kindness that endured in the hearts of her students and bound them together beyond their kindergarten experience. Kindness is like that. We seldom forget an act of kindness done for us, and we always try to reciprocate in some fashion.

LET'S INVITE THE COPS

"Kindness in giving creates love."

~ Lao Tzu

Resiliency literature describes protective factors as those influences that help students overcome the risk factors in their lives. While risk factors such as living in poverty, drug use in the home, or alcoholism in the family tend to promote maladaptive behaviors in youth, protective factors counteract risk factors, tending to increase self-esteem and self-efficacy and promoting healthy development in youth. During adolescence young men and women sometimes find the protective factor of emotional support outside the family, often from a teacher. In their work with at-risk children, Werner and Smith (1992) suggest that some students "had a favorite teacher who had become a role model, friend and confidant for them" (p. 57).

Working successfully with at-risk students requires exceptional insights into the human condition. The following story comes from one of these unique educators, Mr. Mickelson, who works with students from a variety of ethnic backgrounds and challenging family situations. He aims to create a family atmosphere which offers emotional support to his students.

> I think it's important to regularly share a meal with my students so I cook breakfast every Friday for my at-risk kids. They can also invite any adult they want to share breakfast with us. I suggested the school liaison officer would be a good choice so they could meet him on friendly terms first, just in case there was an issue later. And regardless of what they do that week everyone in class comes to breakfast on Friday. I never use Friday breakfast as a punishment no matter what they did that week. This is our time together as a family so no one is ever excluded.

The unconditional nature of the Friday breakfast is one way that Mr. Mickelson provides the emotional support that is lacking in many of his students' lives.

A NOTE

"Anxiety in a man's heart depresses it, but a kindly word makes it glad."
~ Proverbs 12:25

When Kurt walked into class, Mr. Oliver noted an uncharacteristic level of agitation in Kurt's demeanor. Kurt was normally upbeat and talkative, but today he was quietly reticent and seemed to be having an interior dialogue that was clearly troubling. There was a test that day and the students were given ten minutes to do a quick review—what Mr. Oliver calls a "panic review"—prior to taking the test. Mr. Oliver approached Kurt and asked, "Is something bothering you?" Kurt explained that he had been sidetracked the night before, had not studied, and was convinced that he was not going to perform well on the test. Mr. Oliver reassured him, "In class your answers are right on the money. You seem to have a lot of background knowledge here. Rely on that." Mr. Oliver's encouragement didn't seem to have the desired effect. Kurt had taken the designation "panic review" literally and was in anxiety overdrive. Mr. Oliver tells the rest of the story:

> There was something about the frustration he alluded to that, I guess, I just felt compassion for him. I've never done this, but I took a sticky note and I wrote on it, "You CAN do this—you know a lot!" I put this sticky note on the inside of his test. So I handed the tests out and made sure that I gave that one to him. He took it and stuck it on the table next to his test. As I watched he would occasionally take a moment to glance at the note and then go back to writing his test. He got 46 out of 50, so a 92%.

Mr. Oliver recognized a need, addressed it as he thought best, and Kurt performed well. Like so many things we do as teachers, we can't really know the full impact that Mr. Oliver's actions had on Kurt. It would be nice to think that Kurt took the note home, had it framed, and placed it on his mantel, but that did not happen, as Kurt left the note on the desk as he exited the class.

Kurt may have been experiencing an emotional hijacking (Goleman, 1998). The panic he was experiencing, while unusual for him, is experienced by many students. We call it test anxiety. Perhaps the cause of Kurt's test anxiety was the origin of all anxiety: the sense that one is alone. While the words that Mr. Oliver wrote on the paper were encouraging and may have eased Kurt's anxiety, I believe the hidden presence of Mr. Oliver in the note was the supportive factor allowing Kurt to overcome his anxiety and perform well on the test. I suggest that when Kurt intermittently looked at the paper he not only saw the words but also heard Mr. Oliver's voice encouraging him, "You CAN do this! You know a lot!" Encouragement is loving kindness in action.

Letter of Recommendation

"Perhaps I am stronger than I think."

~ Thomas Merton

I have had the privilege of writing hundreds of letters of recommendation for students and teachers. I find this task a humbling experience. Writing a letter of recommendation is a great opportunity to express our admiration while assisting others on their path of success. TyLynn shared her story as she sought to transition from high school to college.

> I know when I was filling out college applications, I didn't know what school I was going to attend because I didn't think I would get into some of the schools that I was most interested in. And then I went back to my math teacher that I had last year and she reassured me to apply, and that I would do really well. She helped me with my applications and even wrote a really, really nice letter of recommendation. I think those are the best things ever to read because they say such nice things that you didn't know that your teachers ever thought about you. Then after I told her that I actually got in she gave me a hug and I just thought that was really nice.

One Phrase

"Love continually elicits, by encouragement, the nascent capabilities of the loved one."

~ Ashley Montagu

Perhaps you can recall when someone, maybe someone you did not even know well, offered an encouraging word that moved you to action or infused you with a confidence that you did not possess.

Angie, a special education teacher, shared an experience from her college days that still influences her today.

> When I was a freshman in college I took the standard English course. I was writing papers with my friends and I was always getting C's for grades. I used to be a really good student and so I thought my writing was just terrible. I didn't have any confidence in my writing all through college. Then I got to my senior year and one of my professors wrote on my paper, "This is perhaps the most profound statement I have ever read from any of my students." And I said to myself, "Oh, my gosh! My writing is profound!" He even stopped me to tell me that personally. Now I'm completely fine with my writing, but all through college it was tough because I had no confidence. One statement made a big difference for me.

IN LOCO PARENTIS

"To teach well, one must love one's pupils as a mother loves a child."

~ Ashley Montagu

It is striking how often parental love comes up in my discussions with teachers and how it is applied. Scientists from many disciplines suggest that parental love is the exemplary model of love because it epitomizes the loving kindness that all of us deserve and through which we flourish. The following insights were offered by teachers who considered the perspective of parental love as vital to their teaching.

Kevin expressed the following insight, common to many of the teachers I interviewed.

> I believe I became a better teacher when I had children of my own. Since having my own children, I always think if it is not good enough for my own children, it is not good enough for my students. If students experience the sort

of love that a parent feels for a child, they will respond in a positive manner. My experience is that when students do not feel that level of love and commitment they shut down, they are not invested in school.

My experience was much the same. When our first child was born, it humbled me to consider the awesome responsibility we all have in nurturing the most precious part of the parents' lives who we serve. As our children grew I became more understanding about the challenges of parenthood. Before we had children, I thought I had all the answers for how to raise kids. After we had children, I realized I didn't know anything.

Benjamin, a high school teacher, describes the kindness and compassion required for both parents and students when working with young adults.

> I think it's important to look at that kid and you try to picture your own child's face there. Maybe that's unfair to teachers who are without children, but that is what I try to do. I know what I think about when I go in for my kids' conferences. They are so precious to me and sometimes I forget that when those parents come to me and they are really concerned about Jr., and I'm thinking about, "Well, you know Jr. forgot to turn this in or that." One of the things you need to do is maybe remember how precious they are to their family.

Penny, an elementary teacher, describes what she wants from her children's teachers and how she applies that approach in her own practice.

> As a parent I have always thought, "I hope they know my child as I know my child." I know that many people see others' children differently. We as teachers need to always remember that this child has qualities that may only be known to his or her parents. We need to always be searching for these qualities. We need to love these children as we know we would want teachers to love our own. As teachers we spend more time than many families

do with these kids. They need our love, acceptance, and kindness."

Shayla, a high school teacher, describes how she tried to mentor a fellow teacher through the perspective of a mother.

> I remember watching a teacher who did not have any children of her own interact with students in a very negative manner. I thought to myself, "She does not know what it is like to have children. She cannot possibly know what it would feel like to have another adult treat her children in that regard." I was always hinting that I always try to treat students like I would want other teachers to treat my own children. I don't know if it ever helped, but that was my intent. But the basic concept to treat all of our students as we would want our children to be treated is certainly a reasonable concept to apply.

Our kindness extends to the parents of our students as well. Sheryl describes how her kindness profoundly impacted a parent.

> I began one conference for a very troubled boy by saying, "Tyler is starting to manage his behavior. I see him stopping and thinking before he reacts. Thanks for working with him on this." The mom immediately burst into tears and told me no one at school had ever said anything positive to her to make her feel good. Not when she was a student, and not since she had become a parent.

Sheryl's story sheds light on why some parents are reluctant to come into our school or approach conferences from a defensive mindset. Sadly, some families have never heard kind words about their children, which may explain why some families have such a low opinion of our schools. We can hope that this mother's perspective about her son's school changed for the better due to Sheryl's loving kindness.

When our own child has a teacher who does not value them, it is a difficult position for any educator. This poses both a personal and professional dilemma. Claudia describes her frustration as both a parent and a colleague based on her daughter's negative experience.

From a parenting perspective it was difficult to have a fellow teacher be hostile toward one of my children. So I have found myself calling this person to task. Her response to me, stated in no uncertain terms, was, "This is how it's going to be, my way or the highway." It was so frustrating. I could put my life experiences right here, little girl. Who do you think you are? And another thing, she has no idea how much I love my child. I wanted to ask her "what have you done that allows you to treat my daughter in such a cold, uncaring fashion?" And the bottom line was I told her, "I feel really sorry for you because in ten years my daughter is going to be doing something and you will have had nothing to do with it. Have you got that figured out?" If you take yourself too seriously, too much of a power play and too much of an importance for what you do in your class, it's going to be a long life—long days, long years, long life.

One can only hope that this teacher heeded the advice of her colleague. What we teach is important, but how we treat our students teaches a far more important lesson.

Evan had a similar experience with his son. While he chose not to confront his colleague, the frustration he shared was very similar to Claudia's.

It's a good experience, I think, as a parent to see when my son, for the first time ever this year, was having conflict with a teacher. What a humbling experience that has been. I see how painful it is for him and I can only imagine how painful it is to be a high school student and have someone not value them because my son does have value to me. No teacher should have the right to trash a student. I've always wanted to tell the teacher, "You don't know him! You don't know how bright he is. Can't you see when he is putting his head down on his desk that you are responsible for what happens to him in that class period?" And yet in high school, students need to start assuming some of their own responsibility too. For some students there are different reasons that they don't seem to care. It's our job to find that out and work with each student as best we can.

A CHRISTMAS GIFT

"The basis of all good human behavior is kindness."

~ Eleanor Roosevelt

It took me a long time to figure out that Christmas break, or for that matter any break from school, was not anticipated with the same delight by all students. For some, Christmas break means that the two meals a day that they could count on may not be there. There may be neither presents nor family fellowship. While heartbreaking, this is simply the fact, particularly in high poverty locations. Students may witness the Christmas spirit on television if they have a television, but they may not experience it in their own lives. For this reason, just before Christmas many schools experience a rise in student misbehavior, which for the unaware, is hard to understand. Students who are generally hardworking and engaged can become apathetic or irritable.

One faculty that it was my privilege to work with was aware of this reality and took steps to address this need. For years the Christmas tradition had been for the Student Council to play the role of Secret Santa for the teaching and support staff. During a faculty meeting it was proposed that we reverse the roles and that each staff member become the Secret Santa for a small group of students so that the entire student body was covered. Each day of Christmas week the Secret Santa left a small gift in their student's locker. The faculty also provided and cooked breakfast each morning for the students. This loving kindness profoundly changed the pre-Christmas break culture. The anxiety experienced by some students dissipated and was replaced by the loving kindness associated with Christmas. Loving kindness is miraculous in its effect, turning anxiety into relief, despair into hope, and isolation into community.

What Students and Teachers Say

"Kindness in words creates confidence. Kindness in thinking creates profoundness."

~ Lao Tzu

We display kindness most commonly through the words we speak. Kind words have a positive influence that stays with students well beyond the moment. As one student told me, "You remember how you were treated, not the grade that you got. You remember what exactly happened, just the little things that stick in your mind. I think what you remember the most and what helps your self-esteem the most and what makes you most confident is just saying, 'That was a good paper,' or 'That was a good job on that problem.' You gain a new confidence when somebody tells you something like that."

Kindness promotes confidence and well-being, allowing each student to manifest the gifts and beauty they possess. Consequently, teachers who consistently demonstrate kindness are the most highly rated teachers by their students (Cothran and Ennis, 2000).

Kindness is also demonstrated through non-verbal communication including appropriate touch. As human beings we naturally respond and are reassured by a warm smile or supportive touch. Betty shared that, "The idea of hugging or putting your arm on a kid's back or tousling their hair, I think that contact recognizes that we are human." Students are grateful when teachers "smile and make you feel welcome when you enter the class," "look at you with kindness—smiling and happy," "pat you on the back as a sign of good faith," and of course "give hugs." There are those who advocate never touching a student; however, there is a time, place, and manner in which touching a student is appropriate and even needed. Having spent a lot of time in elementary schools, I can tell you that young students regularly seek the reassurance of a hug. The start and end of the day is a hug fest in many elementary schools. Students who love their teachers seek a hug when they arrive at school and before heading out the door to go home. Appropriate touch communicates understanding, warmth, support, interest, or approval. Touch is also one of the most important means of communicating psychological and emotional immediacy (Crump, 1996) and a means to promote physical and emotional well-being (Johnson, 1998, Keating, 1983).

Carol, a master educator who has a proven history of bringing out the best in very challenging high school students, thoughtfully describes the power of touch this way.

> Communicating love can be as simple as a pat on the shoulder or arm as you walk by a student. Not just in your own room but anywhere you run into them. Not to catch their attention, just, and I will probably use this phrase again as I go along, but as a "touchstone." Just a quick, wordless reconnection that is an unspoken message of caring.

> This is not always easy with some students who have never experienced physical touches that were not abusive or hurtful. Some students, like some horses, need gentling. Start small and be happy with any successes in that area. Often as the trust continues to build you will find that some students will hug you as they enter or leave the room, grab your hand as they go by, or give you the ever popular high five. This is a part of the touchstone way of thinking that I mentioned before.

> The need to reconnect at difficult and/or random times with something that is strength in their lives is very important to kids. Teenagers today who lead bewildering, media-bombarded, pressure-filled lives, are even more in need of something that is perceived as dependable and consistent to keep them somewhat grounded. A simple touch, although seemingly small, shows caring and appreciation. It is important to kids because we are hard-wired to respond positively to touch.

We make one another feel better or worse based on the emotions we communicate. As much as 90% of emotional communication is transmitted non-verbally through facial expressions, tone of voice, gestures, body movements, and touch. Loving kindness is often communicated non-verbally through a supportive touch or just a smile. "It happens that smiles are the most contagious emotional signals of all, having an almost irresistible power to make other people smile in return. And smiling in and of itself primes positive feelings" (Goleman, 1998, p. 167).

Jennifer describes the power of a supportive touch for the students she works with.

> I think, too, with the at-risk kids we as a team become aware of situations that other people aren't privy to in the building. I know that over the last several years we have had a number of pregnant girls. And boy, those conversations are really hard conversations because they are looking for decisions, they are looking for advice and they don't always know who to talk to. A lot of times they can't talk to a parent because of the pretty rough situations, and sometimes it is just as simple as a touch on the shoulder when they come in the door without words. Lots of times when I'm walking around helping the kids, when I know something about a kid, I will just give them a little hug or something.

A kind touch can be reassuring in ways that words cannot. The message may be as simple as "you are not alone." Angela shares some simple but effective acts of kindness that are appreciated by students as well as parents.

> I send students a "Welcome to My Class" postcard in August before school starts. My hope is that this helps students feel welcomed even before they come for the first day. In years when I taught kindergarten I think that really helped some students who may have been anxious about starting school. Every day I greet students at the door in the morning with a smile and a hello. I also tell them goodbye at the door at the end of the day. I allow kids to choose their method of telling me goodbye with a hug, a handshake, or a high five.

One of the unanticipated responses many teachers shared with me was, "I pray for my students." The surprise was not that teachers pray, or even that many pray for their students. The revelation for me was that so many educators were so forthcoming about their practice and that they did not view it as unique. In fact, several were convinced that it was the kindest act they could do for their students. It occurred to me that, while the practice may be different, the motivation and result would be in line with the research done in the area of self-fulfilling prophecy.

The research on self-fulfilling prophecy exploded on the education scene through the book *Pygmalion in the Classroom: Teacher expectation and pupils' intellectual development* (Rosenthal and Jacobson, 1968). The conclusion of the researchers was that students will generally rise to meet teacher expectations. When we hold an idea in our mind coupled with belief and positive emotion, we tend to act in ways that bring that belief into reality. Perhaps when we pray for our students we are in a sense practicing the Pygmalion Effect by holding only positive impressions in mind when we pray for students. Prayer for others is intercession on their behalf before God. The effect of prayer for students may never be proven, but it doesn't mean that teachers who practice loving kindness through prayer should stop praying for their students if they believe in the benefits.

Kindness is often communicated through praise and encouragement. Burnett (1999), building on previous research, found that praise had a significantly greater influence on achievement than criticism. Praise also resulted in more positive self-talk by students. Commenting on the role of praise, Symonds (1946) writes, "Praise, even in a mild degree, is an expression of love. Children learn most readily in response to love. Anna Freud, for instance, has noted the fact many times verified, that the most important motive for the learning in school is love of the teacher" (p. 564). In the following paragraphs students and teachers discuss loving kindness as expressed in praise, encouragement, concern, and advice.

The following conversation took place between several teachers as they discussed the power of praising students privately rather than publicly. They seem to agree that private, personal praise has the biggest impact on students.

"I remember as a student because it made me feel like a 'puff out my chest' kind of thing. Like when you are in the hall between classes and a teacher whispers, 'Come here. That thing you said today in class—that was great! You were so on with that.' Or, 'That project you turned in, that was quality work right there.' But it was not in the context of the classroom. It was just as you were kind of going down the hall. Or it could have been last night's game or something, but you pull them aside and you take ten seconds to do that and they walk away. I remember as a student, you just feel like you've really accomplished something and it was appreciated."

"How does that compare to something that they have turned in and they got a 100 or 90 out of 100 on it? Clearly they are generally happy with that. How is that different than, and maybe what way is that different than, when you pull them aside and say, 'That was really great—you really hit it on the head—it was logical—it really fell together.' Which one is more valuable?"

"Don't you think the individual one-on-one would be more valuable? When there are other students and you do that in front of the class sometimes they feel embarrassed because it's not the cool thing to do so well. But by doing it one-on-one it really goes back to that whole concept that it's person-to-person. It's not teacher-class, it's not teacher-student, it's person-to-person."

The striking characteristics of this brief conversation are the reflective nature of the participants and the awareness of the needs of the student. Praise is a wonderful thing that we all appreciate, but the time, place, and manner in which it occurs are also important. Praise must be given in a fashion and an environment that fits each student's comfort level.

We tend to praise students for academic success. But many students, like Joey, talk about other attributes for which we praise students and what that means to them.

> Like maybe you aren't good at taking tests, and you can't study very well, and that's why you got a bad grade. But in class you are very inquisitive, you always ask questions, or you are always helpful to other people, but you don't get graded on those things. But when a teacher points it out it makes you feel really good. It encourages and lets me know my work is appreciated. It also encourages me to answer more questions because the teacher tells me, "I'm a bright kid."

Research supports the conclusions of these teachers and Joey. Praise, in order to be effective, should identify specific behavior, include reasons why the behavior is being praised, be credible and done privately most of the time (Brophy, 1981). Blanchard and Johnson (1982) suggest that praise is most effective when it is given immediately, addresses specific behavior, includes the positive effect of the behavior on the person giving the praise, encourages the behavior to continue, and includes acceptable physical contact such as a handshake or a pat on the back.

There is nothing more satisfying to a parent than to have others praise our children. Kim talks about how she shares positive communication with the parents of her students and how much that is appreciated. "I try to send at least one positive postcard home per semester. The notes I write are very simple. 'Dear Mr. and Mrs. Smith, Stuart has worked so hard to learn his ten facts! Keep up the great work.' Also, I always try to start each parent-teacher conference by making an authentic positive comment that acknowledges the parent's efforts and skills. 'Malena is so kind, and that reflects on what I know you're doing at home with her,' or, 'Eli is very empathetic with other kids. You can be so proud of the way he interacts with others at school.'" Kim concludes, "I have had so many parents say, 'We appreciate the fact that you took the extra time to write a nice note about our child. It meant a lot to us as parents.'" Kim shows us the power that small acts of kindness have for everyone.

My own experience as both a teacher and administrator is that when we take the time to pass on our positive observations to parents, parents are much more cooperative if the time ever comes when we need to admonish a student's indiscretion. The kindness we extend to parents makes deposits in their emotional bank accounts (Covey, 1989). If we have made enough deposits, when we need to make a withdrawal we are still metaphorically in the emotional black with the parents we serve. They know that we see the goodness in their child as well as behavior that requires correction.

Kindness is also expressed through concern for the well-being of our students and offering advice when appropriate. Concern begins with the awareness of where students are socially, emotionally, and academically. We take a read on students as they walk the halls or enter our classroom through observing their body language, attitude, and responsiveness. Based on what we observe we may alter our approach or even our entire lesson. In many cases we will pull a student aside and ask if they are doing well. Through expressing our concern, we open a door to further conversation that students can choose to either walk through or close. If the student walks through the door and shares their difficulties, we may offer consolation or advice. It is up to the student to accept or reject what we have to offer. In either case the simple fact that our students know we are aware and concerned for their well-being sends a powerful message that we love them and are available if and when they choose to use us as a resource.

Charlotte, a high school student, shared the following insights about her teachers showing concern and offering advice.

> I think some teachers can tell when you come into class that you are in a bad mood and they come up to you and say, "Hi, how ya doing, is there something wrong?" Or they can tell if students are having problems at home like they aren't clean or are showing like signs of abuse, and asking them if they need help. I was sick one day last year, just one day, and the teachers asked me, "Where were you yesterday?" I told them I was sick, and they missed me and that means they care about me. And that was just one day.
>
> The atmosphere is a huge thing. Like if you are having a bad day, they will recognize it but also talk to you about it. "Hey, if you want to talk about it we can do that; otherwise we're going to take notes." Instead of the teacher prying at you, they just ask and leave it alone if you don't want to talk about it. It's important having people care, knowing that they care, without being pushy. It does comfort you. And even if they do cross that line a little where you really don't want to talk about it, it's kind of alright because it shows that they are actually caring about you. That's a lot better than pretending that they don't see it because it's pretty easy to tell when someone is in a bad mood or different than their normal self.

Charlotte provides sound advice. If we see something that doesn't look right, it doesn't hurt to ask; this is better than ignoring an obviously distressing situation. If the student doesn't want to talk about it, that is their call and we need to respect that. By simply noticing and asking, we demonstrate our concern and care.

Karen, a strong student advocate who works primarily with at-risk students, shares her perspective and experience in addressing sensitive issues with students. She emphasized enrolling the help of other professionals in serving the needs of her students. Just as we never want students to feel alone, we are not alone in helping our students work through tough issues.

> It is important to make sure that students know that what they share with you stays with you. But also make sure that they are aware that some issues you are legally bound to report. When this type of concern comes up I have often had to persuade the student to share their difficulty with their parents, our guidance counselors, or our principal, depending on what the situation is. This is where the trust factor becomes so important. When you explain the importance of sharing with people who have the needed connection to help them, it can give them the strength to do so. Emphasize that, because you love them, you feel that this step needs to be taken to find a solution and start healing.

> I have often gone, by frenzied request, with students for their first conversations with one of these representatives. It is easier for kids when the initial information is put out there by someone else and then they can open up more to begin working through what needs to be done. Then I step back and let these people do what they are so good at doing. If the student wants to talk more after this I am more than happy to continue to be a confidant, knowing that the other wheels are in motion to help them. But time and again without the input and backing of an adult they trust and that they know wants only the best for them, many serious issues would continue to be one of

the little secrets that a child tries to contend with on their own. Before you can reach the point where this trust bond is established, you have to create connections.

I always encourage other adults to not be afraid to approach students who you don't know well, or at all, if they seem to be in distress, unhappy, angry, or sad. If you don't get an answer or you get brushed off, don't take it personally. Showing loving kindness can sometimes be just showing that you care enough to ask.

Kindness can also include attempting to allay student concerns. When a student is anxious about their academic progress, offering advice that looks at the big picture can be a stress reliever. Patrick, a high school science teacher, describes a situation where his advice helped a student relax and focus on the solution rather than the problem.

> I had a student last semester who asked, "You know my midterm grades aren't so good. What does that really mean?" I sensed that she was very concerned so I wanted to respond in a way that relieved some of her stress. I said, "You know, it's just a midterm grade. Really what we are shooting for here is where you are at the end of the semester. You might find out that your first quarter might absolutely stink and that's not where you want to be. But that's not the end all. Your focus should be your semester grade. You might have started slower than you want but if you are going to show some type of progress and demonstrate that you are understanding the concepts, then that's really what we have to go by."

> And that's exactly how I explained it to the student, and she thought that was the greatest thing. At that point I could have pulled the switch the other way and said, "You know, you really are in a tight spot here and you are in a tough situation. You are going to have to buckle down over the next fourteen weeks that you have left or you are going to fail." But the fact that there is concern on her part

to me was a good sign that she is already concerned, so why wouldn't I tell her something that could be a positive?

Kindness can involve the courage and honesty it takes to help students through some tough issues. As a psychology teacher, Peter has the opportunity to talk about many challenging situations that students encounter.

> We always talk a lot in our class about their life because of what we teach. I don't know if you give them advice so much, as you say, "There are going to be some things that will happen as a result of this that you need to be aware of. And this is going to be really difficult on your mom or your dad, more than it is for you. You might have trouble understanding exactly what they are going through. Don't feel you can't talk to them. One of the best ways to deal with this is to deal with it head on." So it's the idea that you are aware that there are things they are going through. You can't put yourself exactly in their place, but be aware of the things that are very unique to them.

Patty shows her loving kindness by giving the same advice and admonition each week as her students leave her class.

> Every Friday as the kids leave my class I shout over the conversation, "Have a good weekend, make good choices. If you get in a car when someone has been drinking, call me." And they always answer back, "We'll be good, Mrs. Johnson." To remind them as a teacher and a mother to make good choices is something I try to do regularly. I want them to be safe. Come back to me on Monday. I always tell them to come back to me on Monday! One week I forgot to do it and they said, "Aren't you going to tell us to behave this weekend?"

What a wonderful message: "Come back on Monday." Jack shares a similar story about Mrs. Schafer.

> One of my colleagues goes through some really interesting situations with some of her students. At the end of the year as they are going into the summer, she wants to make

sure they are safe because for some of those kids that can be the most dangerous time of all. She gives them a card with her name and phone number and tells them to call her if they ever are in a bad situation and need help. She is available for them all the time, and there are kids who have taken her up on that.

Patty's and Mrs. Schafer's willingness to give students their phone numbers and the offer to call them if they get in a tight spot is an unmistakable expression of loving kindness. Some might say this is going too far, but as long as they are comfortable with this practice I commend them. They exemplify a personal loving kindness that far exceeds the norm.

Joanna brings this section to an end by describing an action, but more importantly an attitude, that communicates loving kindness.

I put on a servant-like attitude. You're the teacher, yet, you know they're working on something and they say, "Oh, I've got to go get a scissors." And you say, "I'll go get it for you." That's just part of what you're doing. You are there to encourage and lift them up. They don't see you as sort of a dictator up there but it's someone who is there to serve.

There is no greater calling than to serve through loving kindness.

COACH ANDRIST

"The kindness I have longest remembered has been of this sort, the sort unsaid; so far behind the speaker's lips that almost it already lay in my heart. It did not have far to go to be communicated."

~ Henry David Thoreau

There is an unspoken kindness that communicates from one heart to another, a sensing of one's bond to another, transcending the spoken word. Scientists call this communication limbic resonance. "Within the effulgence of their new brain, mammals developed a capacity we call limbic resonance—a symphony of mutual exchange and internal adaptation whereby two mammals become attuned to each other's inner states" (Lewis, Amini, and Lannon, 2000, p. 63). I was fortunate to have this resonance with Coach Andrist.

Sometimes we feel that we are working harder and are more committed than the students we serve. When this happens, we might feel like we have been let down. As an athlete the surest way to let down your coach and teammates is to not give your best effort. While there are many things outside of our control when we compete, the effort we give is at all times a choice. The only times that Coach Andrist showed disappointment in me was when I failed to give my best effort. Nothing needed to be said because we both knew the truth of the situation. While I sensed Coach's disappointment, I also felt the loving kindness that accompanied it and which was the foundation of expecting only the best I had to offer. He knew I felt badly and he knew why. Why work so hard preparing and then lay down when it really matters? Every athlete for one reason or another has done it. He knew I was just as disappointed in myself as he was in my lack of effort. Nevertheless, I knew in my heart that he loved me and that all his concern was based on his commitment to help me realize my potential.

We sometimes confuse kindness with weakness. Nothing could be farther from the truth. Only a psychologically and spiritually strong person can be kind in situations where anger or disappointment would be expected. Coach Andrist, like all teachers and coaches, was faced with many situations where it was difficult to be kind. In all such situations he proved his strength by choosing to respond with loving kindness.

AVOID DEMEANING LANGUAGE

"Harsh words wound the heart and disturb the soul."

~ Lawrence Lovasik

Demeaning language is the act of unkindness cited most often by students. Teachers and students shared examples of demeaning language that were sad and shocking. "You have the brains of a gnat." "This town is a pile of manure and you are all maggots." "Shut your fat face and turn around." And the especially demeaning, "What do you have, shit for brains?" The result of demeaning language is predictable from a pleasure-pain perspective. Because we tend to avoid painful situations, it is not unusual for students who experience demeaning language to avoid school, dropping out either mentally or physically. Perkins (1965) found that low academic achievement and withdrawal by students was related to harsh criticism received from teachers.

"Maggots"

"I have made a discovery that if you are angry...there's something wrong with you."

~ Anthony de Mello

Imagine you are back in high school. You've just walked into class and your mind is wandering as you take your seat. The teacher begins the class by saying, "This town is a manure pile and you are the maggots." This story is sad but true. If you were subjected to this type of demeaning language, would you be eager to learn?

A gifted and committed master teacher shared this incident with me, but there is more to the story. When asked how the students responded my colleague went on,

> One night the kids went down to his house and he had his car parked in front of his house—he didn't have a garage—it was parked on the side of the street. They took this old beater car they had and they backed into the side of his car. Then they drove around to the front and they backed into the front of his car. Then they drove around to the back and they backed into the back of his car. They smashed it in on all three sides and drove away.

So that was the kind of animosity that existed between the teachers and the students in this district, and it wasn't the only instance before I moved from there.

While not condoning what the students did, one can imagine a student thinking, "Well if he thinks we're maggots, we can sure act that way." I have difficulty believing students would perpetrate a prank like this on a teacher who demonstrated loving kindness rather than contempt.

We don't know if any of these students dropped out of school, but we do know that the toxic atmosphere drove a great teacher out of our profession for several years.

> You know, that was my first teaching job and those were the kind of feelings that existed. It was an adversarial situation in that school. I was there for three and a half years and I got out of teaching and I thought, "If this is the way it's going to be, I don't want any part of it." But then I decided to give it another try and we have a totally different situation here (in his new school district). We do not have that hatred of teachers by students and vice versa.

In this case it was not a student who dropped out, it was a fabulous teacher who thankfully returned to the profession. Unloving teachers don't just harm students; they also harm their colleagues.

An honest assessment shows that there are unkind and incompetent people in the teaching profession just as there are in every profession. The unsettling reality is that an unloving teacher can negatively impact many students over a career and even poison the climate of an entire school. Sometimes the scars left by unloving teachers last for a lifetime. The damage done by demeaning language needs to be recognized, addressed, and eliminated. Teachers who regularly treat students in this fashion must either radically change their behavior or be drummed out of the business. This may sound like an unloving attitude but I suggest it is not. Teachers who are demeaning do not enjoy teaching and too many students suffer as a result. I encourage you to not be an innocent bystander if you witness this type of behavior. Our students and our profession are too important. We are blessed to be in a great profession, it is up to each of us to keep it that way.

A Word of Encouragement

"Kindness adds sweetness to everything. It makes life's possibilities blossom and fills them with fragrance."

~ Lawrence G. Lovasik

Kindness makes our classrooms welcoming, our courses more interesting, and puts our students at ease. In short, kindness creates a great atmosphere for learning. I remember being told as a first-year teacher to "not smile until Christmas." You may have been given similar advice. Thank goodness I did not heed it. If it is still being given, I pity the poor souls who put themselves behind the eight ball by following such bad advice.

Being a model of loving kindness is one of the greatest gifts we offer our students. By embodying loving kindness, we model the path to happiness, fulfillment, and peace: all aspects of the fully actualized life. Our students are always watching, and one of the things they notice, appreciate, and emulate most is our kindness. If we teach nothing else, we must teach kindness because it will open doors for our students that the best education cannot.

Haim Ginott (1972) suggests that only a teacher can "create the emotional climate for learning" (p. 16). Our effectiveness is a function of the emotional climate we create in our classrooms. Ginott suggests, "Every teacher can become aware of the attitudes that alienate, words that insult, and acts that hurt. He can acquire competence and caution in communication, and become less abrasive and less provocative" (p. 27). In other words, we can learn to be kind in all situations.

Our effectiveness is also a function of our communication. Our language must emphasize acceptance rather than rejection. This enhances a student's confidence and self-esteem. Ginott writes, "To a large extent, their (teachers') language determines his (students') destiny" (p. 82). The worst communication is perceived as a judgment of the student's character or personality. The cardinal rule of communication is to address the situation, not the student's character. Condemn the act, not the actor. Ginott emphasizes the importance of communication when he writes, "Yet words can brutalize as well as civilize, injure as well as heal. Teachers, like parents, need language of compassion. A language that lingers lovingly" (p. 211). Loving language is rooted in kindness.

"A tree is known by its fruit; a man by his deeds. A good deed is never lost; he who sows courtesy reaps friendship, and he who plants kindness gathers love."

~ St. Basil

PART II

Professional Connection

PART II
· · · · · · · · · · · · ·

Professional Connection

"In a sense love fills us with knowledge, because co-participation and co-experience is the richest experience of all the generations of humanity…Love is the most efficient method of learning and the most fruitful way to truth and knowledge."

~ Pitirim Sorokin

As the personal connection is the gateway to a student's heart, the professional connection is the pathway to the mind. For some students it is important to first capture their hearts, to build personal connections. For others, stirring the mind through the love of knowledge—loving what we do—is more important. For others it is the charismatic connection, connecting through the core of our being, which ignites the imagination of the student. Because of the unique character of each teacher and student there is no formula or pattern to follow. Each connection is a manifestation of love and each student will be drawn to that which most readily matches their nature and needs. In an ideal world we bond with our students through all three connections. But this is not an ideal world, so we work to influence our students in the best way we can. Each of the three connections can be the doorway leading to the others.

To educe—draw forth from students that which lies within them—is an intensely human interaction. For thousands of years we have learned from one another through imitation, the exchange and challenge of ideas, and experiencing the world through others' eyes. Meaningful learning takes place at the nexus of the exposure to new

ideas or experiences and the interaction of human minds questioning, analyzing, reflecting, applying, and creating. The professional
connection through which we seek to discover and understand truth,
beauty, and goodness is, at its core, a person-to-person endeavor.
As teachers we are both leaders and guides, providing our students
with meaningful and challenging experiences while at the same time
providing the support and guidance they need to master the knowledge and skills we are pursuing.

Kim, an elementary teacher, describes beautifully the part that
love plays in the professional connection.

> Love changes everything! The "end" I envision for my
> students is one in which they have become good-hearted
> people with strong character, avid readers, competent
> problem solvers, and enthusiastic lifelong learners. I
> know, however, that those things don't just happen in an
> individual's life. I must enthusiastically teach and model
> those skills and behaviors I hope to see in my students.
> But without a platform of love, good instruction has no
> place to land.

It is love that supplies learning with meaning, relevance,
context, and application to students' lives. Only a fellow human
being, one mind and heart to another, can make this happen. While
information can be transferred through a book, a video, an iPad,
or a computer, true learning is internalized through experience and
participation with other human beings.

One of the most meaningful learning laboratories we have is
the natural beauty of the wilderness. Learning can and should feel
like an adventure into the wilderness where the teacher acts as the
guide indicating where to go and occasionally suggesting how to get
there. It is the student's responsibility to choose whether, and sometimes how, to make the passage. The student must carry their pack,
help set up and break down camp, start the fire for cooking, wash the
dishes, and all the rest of the duties associated with an expedition.
In short the student must do the bulk of the work. When new challenges are presented the teacher suggests options for addressing the
challenges: run the rapids or portage, follow the switchbacks or head

straight over the mountain, rappel the cliff or walk two days around. The guide works hard to provide a meaningful challenge along with the support for his fellow adventurers. The adventure, like learning, is based on the co-participation of the teacher and the student.

A great guide in the wilderness or the classroom gives his best, is willing to provide all the assistance required, and provides meaningful challenges while maintaining high expectations of his fellow adventurers. The guide understands that each individual is endowed with unique capabilities, interests, and aversions, and working with these distinctive characteristics the guide meets each adventurer where they are on their journey. The characteristics of a successful guide apply as much to an assault on Mount Everest as they do to teaching students how to read. When these assets are in place students are naturally drawn to the pursuit of truth, beauty, and goodness. Great teachers are great guides.

"In this sense love-experience leads to a true cognition, and love transforms itself into truth and knowledge. In these two ways the power of love reinforces the power of truth and knowledge."

~ Pitirim Sorokin

Chapter Four:
Give Our Best

WHY GIVING OUR BEST IS LOVE AND WHY IT MATTERS

"Teachers believe they have a gift for giving; it drives them with the same irrepressible drive that drives others to create a work of art or a market or a building."

~ Bartlett Giamatti

Giving lies at the heart of both teaching and loving. This is one of the reasons why we suggest that teaching, by its nature, is an act of love. Through giving we aspire to enrich the lives of our students. In ancient Hebrew texts the word love is depicted by two characters which literally translate into "I give." Giving lies at the very heart of what it means to be a loving person and consequently a loving teacher, expecting nothing in return because giving is pure delight.

Erich Fromm in his classic work *The Art of Loving* (1956) describes how and why we give as loving human beings.

> He gives of himself, of the most precious he has, he gives of his life…he gives of him that which is alive in him; he gives him of his joy, of his interest, of his understanding, of his knowledge, of his humor, of his sadness—of all expressions and manifestations of that which is alive in him. In thus giving of his life, he enriches the other person, he enhances the other's sense of aliveness, by enhancing

his own sense of aliveness. He does not give in order to receive; giving is in itself exquisite joy (p. 23).

This is one of the most accurate descriptions of what it means to be a loving teacher, giving everything we have to enrich the lives of our students, because through this act we experience exquisite joy.

Giving can be very difficult, requiring us to rise above self-centered desires. Mother Teresa suggests that in order to truly love we must "give until it hurts." As I look at the professionals I have worked with over the years, this is exactly what really great teachers are willing and able to do.

Giving our best requires having high expectations of ourselves prior to formulating high expectations for our students. In order for our students to perform better, we first need to get better. Too often in my own career it was easy to see my students' rather than my own shortcomings as the problem. They weren't motivated, didn't study or take good notes, weren't prepared for class, wouldn't engage in learning, were gone too often—you know the drill. It was not until I took a good hard look at myself and expected more from myself, that my practice and consequently student achievement improved. As Dr. Stephen Covey (1989) suggests, if we think the problem is out there, that very thought is the problem.

Because love and teaching are about giving, we need to continually add to the bag of gifts we offer. We can't give away what we don't have. For myself there was a big difference between what I initially had to offer students and what I was able to provide later in my career. We can improve our practice by broadening our knowledge base, varying techniques, working on more effective classroom management, leveraging the use of technology, and building more effective relationships with students, parents and colleagues. The opportunities for improvement are infinite.

Most students do not fail in school because they are incapable of doing the work. Most students who fail do so because they have not developed the habits required to succeed. As classroom leaders, giving our best is one of the most valuable attributes we can model for our students. Students are always watching what we do and taking cues from the messages we send. If we take a day off, the message is that giving our best effort is optional. If we are late for class, we model that punctuality is not important. If we are not fully prepared for class, we cannot expect anything different from our students. If we want our students to be prepared, inquisitive, diligent, and reliable, we need to model all of these attributes. What we model is what we can expect and what we will get from our students.

Witnessing students not living up to their God-given potential is heartbreaking. Many students have bought into the quick fix mentality promoted throughout our culture. It is more convenient to take steroids than to spend time in the weight room. Buying endless lottery tickets is the quick and easy way to achieve financial independence. These are some of the lies that our culture sells to our students every day—that there is a shortcut to every success. We must act as a bulwark against this deception by modeling what it means to give our best every day. In each of the following stories you will find teachers who expected the best from themselves.

"This Is Boring."

"The curious paradox is that when I accept myself just as I am, then I can change."

~ Carl Rogers

As a student teacher, I had a minuscule tool box of teaching strategies. In fact, I had only four tools: lecture, discussion, worksheets, and movies, with lecture being my long suit. That was it. Discussions were interesting but short-lived because, God forbid, a student might ask a question I couldn't answer. This included almost any question worth asking. I was like the carpenter who had only a hammer in his tool box. To me, everything looked like a nail. The only tool change at my disposal was a bigger hammer. The wakeup call came one day when a very bright student in the front row accurately declared, "This is boring." He said it under his breath so as not to make a scene, but loud enough so I could hear him. He was right. He was my teacher that day because he taught me that being boring is worse than being bored. I never wanted to be boring again. I had to enlarge my tool box, step out of my comfort zone and grow. I needed to have higher expectations of my teaching skills, and accept the fact that I had to change to be effective. I suppose I was giving the best I had to offer at the time, but that was clearly not what my students deserved. Giving our best includes growing professionally throughout our career until the day we retire. No glide paths allowed.

"I KNOW NOTHING."

"If there is anything we wish to change in the child, we should first examine it and see whether it is not something that could better be changed in ourselves."

~ Carl Jung

My knowledge base in my first year of teaching is best described through the famous words of Sergeant Schultz from "Hogan's Heroes": "I know nothing." I graduated with a broadfield social studies degree, which in a practical sense meant that I knew very little about a lot of subjects. Ostensibly I was equipped to teach all history subjects (World, American, African, Asian, European, Middle Eastern, Ancient, Modern, etc.), psychology, sociology, anthropology, economics, government and geography. The truth was that my expertise in most of these areas was very thin, even anorexic.

A few weeks after graduating from college, I secured my first teaching job. I didn't ask, and the folks who hired me never mentioned, what I would be teaching. I had a social studies degree and could coach two sports; that seemed to be good enough for them so it was good enough for me. I was in way over my head but was too naive to realize it.

Sometime during the middle of the summer I learned that I would be teaching psychology, sociology and Native American history. If I had to pick three subjects that I was licensed to teach but woefully ill-equipped to teach, these three would have been at the top of the list. I had never even read a book about Native American history and had only taken the minimum number of credits in psychology and sociology. I didn't find either subject particularly engaging so I considered attendance at these classes as optional, very optional. My shortcomings in these areas were self-inflicted wounds because I had not paid the price in studying. I had a lot of catching up to do.

Most teachers have been in this predicament at some point in their career. They have taught a subject, coached a sport, or sponsored an activity that, for any number of reasons, they were ill-prepared to take on. My student teaching supervisor, Mr. Keith, was a master teacher, but when he started teaching he told me that he skipped certain chapters in the text because he had no idea what they were talking about. I can tell you Mr. Keith, after thirty years of teaching experience, was a master of both his subject area and his craft.

I spent most of the summer reading and studying but remained well behind the curve when I showed up for my first professional job. Throughout the school year I typically came home after practice and stayed up until midnight preparing for the next day's lessons. The good news is that I think I was an adequate teacher on most days because I had finally paid the price. Certainly there were days that were busts. I share these two examples from my own experience to illustrate that for my students to do better, I had to get better.

"THIS ISN'T GETTING THE HAY IN THE BARN."

"'You are happy.' The true ethics whisper.
'Therefore you are called upon to give much.'"

~ Albert Schweitzer

Giving our best includes freely giving of our time for those we serve. While time is the most important commodity we have, something we can never get back, it is also the most valuable asset we have to share. Kevin, a master agricultural teacher and Future Farmers of America advisor, shares his experience regarding his mentor.

When I was a student, I think what affected me most was having a teacher willing to give up their time—evenings,

Saturdays, weekends, vacation time—to do things with us in various activities. I guess maybe that's one reason why I do what I do with the kids because I know how it impacted me and I want to provide that same impact. You know, take students places, do things with them, give them experiences that they wouldn't have in a normal classroom setting. Being an educator was not my first choice. I worked in business for a number of years before I started teaching. I realized I wasn't having the impact with adults that I thought I could have on kids. So that's why I decided to go into teaching.

Kevin takes his students to every convention and workshop available, along with camping, white water rafting, jet skiing, and cycling all over the Midwest. By giving his time, Kevin not only enriches the lives of his students, he enriches his own life. Giving his best means freely giving that which is most precious to him: his time.

"WHY DOES 5+5=10?"

"Setting an example is not the main means of influencing another, it is the only way."

~ Albert Einstein

Blake, a high school student, describes Mr. Harrison as one who goes the extra mile not only in generously sharing his time, but also in making sure that students understand the all-important question—why?

Mr. Harrison is always at school by 6:00 or 6:30 in the morning and he stays there until 4:00 or 5:00 every single day. I think that shows how much he enjoys teaching. When I realize I've learned something new, that's the whole point of teaching. With Mr. Harrison you really think and learn why you are learning it because you learn the concept behind things. Some classes are 5 + 5 = 10 because that's how it always is and you just need to know that. Mr. Harrison teaches everything more in depth. He explains how you take 5 and take another 5 and then how and why that becomes 10. It's not just about random facts. He gets into the concept so that you really understand it. You need to know that for your life. He wouldn't just tell you 5 + 5 = 10. He asks if you have 5 and then another 5, you tell me what happens. Most teachers don't take that kind of time to make sure you really understand.

Teaching "random facts," preparing kids to appear on Jeopardy, is easy to do but of little consequence. When we expect more of ourselves and commit to teach for mastery and full understanding, as Mr. Harrison models for us, then we have truly educated our students.

WHAT STUDENTS AND TEACHERS SAY

"The man who sets about making others better is wasting his time, unless he begins with himself."

~ St. Ignatius Loyola

The following conversation reveals the expectations these teachers have for themselves and how, through meeting these expectations, they give their best. They revolve around five main ideas: understanding the learning process, having a robust knowledge base, maintaining high expectations of our own conduct as real models, being willing to give of our time, and effective classroom management skills. All of these traits take time and commitment to develop, and the more we develop in these five areas the more we have to give away.

"I could be wrong, and this may have more to do with high school students, but when I think of the people that students respect, they respect a certain amount of knowledge. If I am up there teaching but I am not helping them to fulfill their academic goals, I am not doing my job. I started out as a middle school teacher, and when I went to the high school one of my friends said, 'You can't do that, you are too good with middle school kids.' But I think I'm much better with high school kids because the kids realize that I put a lot of effort into understanding my content and am able to explain it. They respect that I am able to help them achieve a certain level academically."

"I think as teachers we need to know lots of different areas. I think you need to be an expert in your area but I see so many teachers that don't have knowledge of other areas. Not that I think they should have gone through four years of college majoring in everything, but a general lack of knowledge comes across to students as well. When you've gone through four years of college, you should be able to do a basic math operation, you should be able to know where a few of the commas go, something about literature and those types of things."

"What he's saying, I think, is there are people who get tunnel vision in their content area and that's all they see and that's all they understand. I think you need two things; you need a broad general knowledge to show that you are an educated person. But I think you also need to demonstrate a strong expertise in your subject area. When I have been honored enough to go to these Excellence in Education banquets, what strikes me when I look at my colleagues from other schools that I know, and there are two that I can think of particularly at our school who have taught my son, they have very, very high demands but also have such a strong knowledge base. They communicate what the expectation is and they know their material. So when I listen to these kids and why they pick their favorite teacher, it isn't always because they made them feel warm and fuzzy. These are top level students generally. But these are students who admired that teacher and that relationship because that teacher pushed them and that teacher was able to give them everything they were able to absorb."

"I think it's holding up a standard and then not backing down. That's how I think that they understand that I care for them, by holding them accountable and sticking to it. That starts with me holding myself accountable. There are some things that have to be done a certain way. You are willing to be patient and withstand whatever they try to do to get you to change your standards."

"A lot of what we are talking about boils down to priorities and how we use our time. Taking the time to reinforce our expectations or deal with a behavior issue when what we really want to do is stick with our lesson plan. Working with a student who comes in on your prep hour when you are trying to finish up a test. Taking the time to make a phone call to a parent. All of these things are important but they just take time."

It is interesting how this conversation ended with the topic of time. Time is one of the hardest things to give up, but it is also the thing that students want the most. In seeking our time, what students are really saying is they want us. That should be a flattering realization. Billy described his desire this way. "Being willing to meet with students any time to help them. Whether it's coming in early, skipping lunch, or staying late. Just the willingness to almost be on call for students."

When we spend extra time with a student and are patient in persisting with instruction until they fully understand the concept, we are giving our best. Jamie, a mid-school student, describes how a teacher giving up their time makes her feel. "The teacher lets you think about it and helps you get it, and she's really patient, and you can tell like, even if I need to go over the answer like four times, she sticks with it—it feels good."

The wide variation in time that individual students need to experience the productive struggle to fully understand a concept is one of the variables that make teaching so challenging. Patience and persistence are both hallmarks of effective teaching and loving behavior.

When going the extra mile to help our students it is important that they never feel like they are a burden. From his high school experience Eric recalls, "There is nothing worse than feeling like you're a nuisance when you need help. As a student I remember that and it makes you feel crappy. You never want to go get help again, and you're not real fond of that teacher after that." Projecting an invitational manner encourages our students to ask for the help they need.

Mr. Harvey had many admiring and appreciative students. In this discussion some of Mr. Harvey's students describe the professional connection they had with him, as well as the positive impact he had on his students.

> With Mr. Harvey, when you go in and ask for help, one of the things that I like most is that he sits down and, even if he's writing a test that he has to give next hour and he has fifteen minutes left and he's not going to finish it, he'll put everything else down and come and sit next to you. Rather than just saying, "Well, this is the answer and this is how you go about it," he'll figure it through with you and it's almost like he is learning it himself. He takes suggestions from you, like if you suggest something and he knows it's wrong he won't say, "No, that's wrong, this is how you should do it." He'll try it my way. He just treats you like more of an equal than any other teacher.

Other students describe how Mr. Harvey went the extra mile to pursue an interest that they had.

> We told Mr. Harvey once that we were really interested in learning about wild mushrooms in the area. He had a mushroom unit—fungus, it grows on dead animals—how exciting could that be? Anyway, we told him we wanted to learn about it and asked him if he would help us. He said, "Well, I have to work until 4:00 but I am free after school on Wednesday." We didn't have track practice on Wednesday so that worked for everyone. He got one of the school vans and a bunch of us got together and he called it an ecology field trip. He took his own time to drive us out to the woods where we hunted for a couple hours looking for mushrooms. Even when we didn't find any he'd always find something interesting. "Here's a rattlesnake orchid—look at the veins on the leaf—that's how you identify them. If you grind them up and add this

to it, you can make poison." He was really excited about it. He even made fungus seem really interesting.

When we give of our time and can even make fungus interesting, we have made the professional connection with our students.

Coach Andrist

"When we do the best we can, we never know what miracle is wrought in our life, or in the life of another."

~ Helen Keller

Coach Andrist came from very humble beginnings in rural Minnesota but still found a way to put himself through college. He then took an anemic wrestling program and turned it into a championship caliber program which produced college level athletes. He aspired to teach and coach at the college level and did so successfully, mentoring many national champions and place winners. He intended to be a school administrator and achieved that dream while earning an advanced degree. Coach Andrist went into private enterprise, becoming a successful entrepreneur owning and operating his own hotel as well as raising and racing thoroughbred horses.

There was nothing that Coach Andrist expected from others that he did not do himself many times over. He never sought the easy road; if his motel needed a new roof he replaced it himself. All of the attributes that made Coach Andrist successful in these endeavors were evident in his teaching and coaching career. As a coach he worked to be more knowledgeable in his craft, attending every coaching clinic available and then using that knowledge in building successful young men. He continues to coach as well as work diligently on his ranch in Arizona. Because of his impeccable reputation he was recently coaxed out of retirement to take over as principal of an ailing elementary school. Coach Andrist has experienced a life of fulfillment and achievement. The foundational attribute to Coach Andrist's success is that he always gives his best.

AVOID QUITTING

"Make the most of yourself, for that is all there is of you."
~ Ralph Waldo Emerson

There is a substantial difference between being a teacher and an instructor. The attitude of the instructor is, "I did my job, I presented the material, whether you understand it or not is not important to me. The test is Tuesday and I don't really care one way or the other how you do, that is your concern, not mine." Instructors believe that all they need to do is present information and they have done their job. A book, computer, or video can instruct, that is, transfer information, but only a fellow human being can teach, that is, make learning a personal, interesting, and meaningful experience. On rare occasions some of our colleagues commit one of the most egregious derelictions of duty when they simply quit teaching. It is difficult to understand why someone would simply quit teaching, but it happens.

Cory, a high school teacher, describes an experience he had in high school.

> I look back to my high school chemistry teacher and I will never forget what she told us on one of the first days of class. She said, "If you don't get something the first time I explain it to you, you are on your own. You are a stepping-stone for me to teach at the college level and that's the only reason I'm here." Well, needless to say, I learned chemistry from my geometry teacher. I really didn't go to her for help, and she was that way with every one of us. From that point on chemistry to me was a negative. I hated the subject. I didn't want anything to do with it.

Frank shares a similar story from his high school experience.

> I had a geography teacher that was awful. He was a man who smoked and chewed and would leave our class to go take a smoke break outside. We all knew where he was going. And he didn't talk to us—literally, he would

grunt—and yes and no were the only things we heard him say. We got packet upon packet of maps to color. I'm a history teacher but I'm awful with geography, however, I'm really good at coloring. I'm great at staying in the lines, I always have been. I got an A from him and I didn't learn a thing, but I could color maps. The less you bothered him the better your grade.

I heard this same, sad lament from Connie, a high school junior, who shared the following regarding her experience of coloring for grades.

All we did was color maps. It's supposed to be a social studies class, it wasn't even geography. We wouldn't go over any of the chapters but we'd have all of these huge tests with questions we didn't even learn about. How were we supposed to know all of this if all we did was color maps?

If our students' educational experience consists of busy work such as coloring maps, we will lose them if we have not lost them already. Boredom is a greater menace to our students than being challenged beyond their abilities. No matter what challenges you are facing please don't quit; don't give up on our students. They deserve the best we have to offer.

A WORD OF ENCOURAGEMENT

"If you are successful you will win some false friends and true friends; succeed anyway."

~ Mother Teresa

When we enthusiastically give our best every day we will be admired by some and scorned by others. There are those in every profession who try to pull us down to a norm of mediocrity. Some imply that your hard work is making them look bad, but the truth is that their own average or poor work is making them look average or poor; it has nothing to do with you. I have seen this in many settings, and I am sure you have, too. The herd can get nervous when one of its number gets too far out in front. Even educators occasionally try to reel in a high flier who, in their mind, may be experiencing too much success.

The best advice on the market is to not be overly influenced by either admirers or critics. We can assume that both are well intentioned, but neither is likely to be aware of our unique situation, motivation, or ultimate aim. While we tend to appreciate admiration and avoid criticism, each can inhibit our development. An addiction to admiration and praise can imprison us to mindless repetition of behavior in the hopes of garnering continued praise not because what we do is useful, but simply because it garners praise. Criticism can cause us to be too self-conscious and, out of fear, second guess every move we make. Angst of this type can make our professional lives miserable. Both the admirer and the detractor can inhibit our development as we strive to give our best every day. Give your best effort in either case without paying too much attention to either admirers or detractors.

"Perhaps the most valuable result in education is the ability to make yourself do the thing you have to do, when it ought to be done, whether you like it or not."

~ Walter Bageh

Chapter Five:
Expect the Best

Why Expecting the Best Is Love and Why It Matters

"In the sphere of human relations, faith is an indispensable quality of any significant friendship or love…having faith in a person refers to the faith we have in the potentialities of others."

~ Erich Fromm

Expecting the best is typically stated in educational jargon as having high expectations for our students. In terms of human love, expecting the best is grounded in the belief and faith that each individual possesses unique gifts which they are eager to discover, develop, and employ (Maslow, 1971). Belief refers to conviction based on discernible evidence while faith is having that same conviction despite any discernible evidence. The leap of faith makes having high expectations an act of love for teachers. The faith of just one interested adult can make all the difference in a child's life. Faith encourages students to push beyond their often times limited perception of their abilities into horizons yet unknown. Faith is the love that says, "Despite anything in your personal history, I believe in you, and I will not abandon you until you have discovered your strengths." Most of us have been fortunate to have someone in our lives whose expectations for our achievement exceeded our own, someone who would not let us settle for mediocrity. They loved us in a way that, while it may have seemed hard at the time, led us to the accomplishments that best define who we are as human beings. We have a choice to provide either high or low expectations. High expectations communicate confidence in the inherent abilities of our students and influence student confidence, achievement, and attribution for success. Low expectations have the opposite impact (Barnard, 1995).

When we believe in our students, which is simply the belief that all human beings have a natural tendency to actualize potential (Maslow, 1971), they seldom disappoint. Simple belief compels us to act in ways that tend to bring that belief into reality. When we believe in ourselves academically, we study diligently and generally to good effect. But when we don't believe in our academic ability, we procrastinate and studying seems like a waste of time. When we believe in our athletic abilities, we practice hard in order to get better. When we don't believe in our athletic abilities, we may still practice but not with the same intensity of purpose as when we believe.

When we believe in our students, we provide them the freedom to believe in themselves. When the people we respect believe in us, their assurance compels us to act in ways that lead to success. The maxim, "I'll believe it when I see it," needs to be abandoned and replaced with, "When I believe it I will see it."

"WHEN ARE YOU GOING TO START THINKING?"

"When we learn to ask good questions, we discover yet another competence is needed: the ability to turn a question-and-answer session between the teacher and the individual student into a complex communal dialogue that bounces all around the room."

~ Parker J. Palmer

As a young student I thought being educated consisted in remembering what I read and what the teacher told me, and being able to repeat it back when asked to do so. It never occurred to me that being an educated person required thinking. I wonder if our students regard schooling in the same fashion. How many times has a student said, "Just tell me what you want me to know?" We seem to have trained our students to believe that learning is an exercise in memorization.

It wasn't until my senior year in high school that Mr. Hubbard, a grizzled but wise social studies teacher, looked at me with an interesting combination of bewilderment and disgust and asked, "Mr. Nolan, when are you going to start to think?" Having never been formally asked by a teacher to think I didn't know what to say. I could recall facts, perform computations, conduct an experiment and report findings, copy out of the encyclopedia, and play dodge ball pretty well. That seemed to have gotten me this far without any trouble. Think? Mr. Hubbard had apparently asked a question that required more than the parrot-type answer I had learned to supply: the right answer according to what the teacher wanted to hear. I was totally unprepared to respond. Thankfully, Mr. Hubbard didn't settle for a canned response. He expected more.

What we learned from our experience with Mr. Hubbard was the joy of thinking. I also learned that my classmates had a lot of very interesting perspectives that I had never considered. Mr. Hubbard was the master questioner and provocateur of dialogue and thought. The challenge of his class (American government) made it enjoyable. I also learned that thinking is really hard. At first I just offered my opinions, confidently assured that I was right. But Mr. Hubbard didn't particularly care how I felt about an issue if I couldn't back it up with evidence to substantiate my position. He instinctively knew that questions which promote sustained thinking result in much more learning (Garmston, 2000) and that high level questioning promotes creativity (Runco et al., 1998). Many times I came away from his class frustrated by my inability to justify a position with facts. This spurred me to do my research so that I could go back to class the next day and "win" through unequivocally justifying my position. Thankfully, Mr. Hubbard expected enough of his class that we began to get a real education when he required us to think.

MY FIRST GIG

"How many activities can you count in your life that you engage in simply because they delight you and grip your soul? Find them out, cultivate them, for they are your passport to freedom and love."

~ Anthony de Mello

As educators we are all blessed with the freedom to do what we love, because we love what we do. My love for history began in the summer between my eighth grade and freshman years when I went to see my oldest brother, Tom, in Maryland. We spent much of our time at museums and historical sites throughout the northeast. The most powerful experience for me was the day we spent at Gettysburg National Battlefield. We got there early and stayed late. I was captivated by the experience of walking on Cemetery and Seminary Ridge, Big and Little Round Top, Spangler's Spring, and of course, The Angle. That was the day that history came to life for me and became a very personal experience, an experience I wanted to, out of sheer joy, share with others. I still wonder if I would have had the courage to cross that field on July 3, 1863, as those Confederate soldiers did, marching into the withering fire from the Army of the Potomac.

My United States history teacher, Mr. Peterson, was a wonderful man who shared my new found passion for history. When we got to the Civil War unit he asked me to give a talk about my experience at Gettysburg. I was anxious to do it, but what was he thinking? I was a freshman in high school, for crying out loud! As you have already read, I had one teacher who thought I was a pinhead. What a contrast! "Darth Vader" had no faith in me, but Mr. Peterson surely did. He said, "Gerry, you know this material better than I do, you teach the class." Mr. Peterson's faith in me was the start of my teaching career. There was no evidence that my presentation would be done well, but that did not seem to matter to Mr. Peterson; he had faith in me.

I spent a lot of time making big colorful maps illustrating each day of the three-day battle. My brother worked for the Department of Defense so I could get accurate information. I read every book and pamphlet I could get my hands on, really trying to prepare well. When the day came I got up in front and started talking, pointing to maps, showing pictures, asking and answering questions, and generally trying to make it a good time for all. It was a delightful experience.

I suppose Mr. Peterson thought I would talk for ten or fifteen minutes and sit down. Well, I talked that whole hour, taking questions from my fellow students and well-timed questions from Mr. Peterson. My sense is that he asked questions when he thought it was getting a little dry. He never said, "Well, that's enough, Gerry, thank you for the presentation." He let me go the whole hour.

I am not sure what the other students got out of this talk, but for me it was a life-changing experience. Mr. Peterson, by expecting a great deal from me, gave me my first shot at what became my life's work. His leap of faith provided me the freedom to do what I loved.

The Risk Worth Taking

"No man is free who is not master of himself."

~ Epictetus

Mr. Riley describes the practices of his colleague Mr. Cain, who, by giving students significant responsibilities, brought out the best in even the most challenging students. Year after year Mr. Cain's students not only met expectations, they exceeded them.

Our drama teacher, Mr. Cain, has for thirty years, and more times than one can remember, taken a kid who has driven everybody else crazy and turned them around by making that kid the stage manager, lighting manager, or put them in charge of stage craft for the school plays. Kids that you didn't think had an ounce of responsibility would tell him to go away, that they could handle it. They told him they would have everything done and son of a gun they did. They had it done well and responsibly. I have seen these kids become very important people in our community as first responders, law enforcement, and medical professionals. They have become very responsible adults because of their experience with Mr. Cain through our drama program.

When we show faith in students, particularly students who have a checkered past, we must expect warnings, second guesses, or even ridicule from our colleagues. Well-meaning colleagues thought that Mr. Cain was foolish to expect the best from students whose history did not inspire confidence. Labeling students as unreliable blinds us to the innate abilities that each possesses. Mr. Cain saw these students through the eyes of faith and love, seeing the inherent potential residing in each student.

"HONESTY IS THE BEST POLICY."

"Charity and kindness unwedded to truth are not charity and kindness, but deceit and vanity."

~ St. Ignatius Loyola

According to Josh, a high school student, expecting the best should also apply to the grades earned by students. Students know when they have earned a grade based on rigorous expectations and when they have been assigned a grade based on some other criteria. To expect less than a student's best effort is insulting, counterproductive, and sends the wrong message.

> I respect teachers when you are graded really honestly. When you are consistently getting C's, it's not really great, but then you get an A or a B and you really know that you did a good job on it. There are some classes where you really don't have to do anything; you just get a good grade anyways. It really doesn't mean anything to you. You can just tell when you have done something well.

WHAT STUDENTS AND TEACHERS SAY

"The only way someone can be of help to you
is in challenging your ideas."

~ Anthony de Mello

Charlotte, a high school student, offers her perspective on the topic by emphasizing the need for students to have high expectations of themselves.

> It really helps when teachers talk to us about our goals too, that we push toward setting and following through on them. It's important that teachers talk about our own responsibilities. Today Mrs. Smith handed our quizzes back and some people didn't do so hot on it and she was saying about how, "You know, if you think you're going to fail, then you will fail. I think if you have more confidence in yourself then you will do better on the test." I think that's true—and I think that kind of helps us pump up for the next test. She tries to get you to become the best you can by expecting more of you.

Jim suggests that when we believe in our students it "allows you to grow more as a human being because if one person believes in you, you should believe in yourself." Jamie observes that many students work hard when they see their teachers work hard because, "It makes me want to make them proud. So I work harder so that they have a reason to believe in me. I don't want to let down a teacher who believes in me so I work extra hard to succeed for myself, which is also a victory for them." Jamie eloquently describes the reciprocal nature of love in action. When we have high expectations of ourselves and our students, everyone gets on board and everyone is a winner.

Having high expectations for students is often communi-cated through loving, supportive, expectant language. The follow-ing examples come from Mrs. Pike, an elementary teacher. There are no confrontations or threats, just a supportive teacher who reminds students that they are capable and responsible for their actions.

"Long division is hard, but I know you can do it, Becca! Just look how smart you are at double-digit multiplication and that was hard in the beginning too!"

☖

Nate: "Mrs. Pike, will you zip my coat"

Mrs. Pike: "Let me see you try first, Nate."

Nate: "Oh, I got it!"

Mrs. Pike, smiling: "Sometimes it just helps to stand next to your teacher!"

☖

Matti: "I don't know what to do."

Mrs. Pike, smiling: "You're going to have to give me more clues. What do you need help with?"

Matti: "I can't read this word."

Mrs. Pike: "No problem! It says *underline*. Now can you keep going?"

Matti: "Yep!"

☖

In expecting the best it is important to not rescue our students, but to allow them to experience reality in the form of a productive struggle and natural consequences. When we rescue students, we send a clear message that students are incapable of solving their own problems which creates dependency. Please notice the grace with which Mrs. Pike lovingly communicates both the parameters and the consequences of the students' choices in the following examples.

"Autumn and Austin, when you are done at the art center it's your job to clean it up in time for recess." (Autumn and Austin do not get the job done.)

"Autumn and Austin, you'll need to spend your recess time cleaning and organizing the art center since you didn't do it at center time."

△

"If you're talking during word wall bingo, you'll lose the chance to play with us today." (One of the students doesn't comply.)

"Olivia, it's a bummer you can't keep playing word wall bingo with us today. But you can try again next week!"

△

"Grady, I see you've been having trouble finding a spot at the carpet that is a good choice for you. That means I get to make the choice instead; so you will sit right here next to me for the rest of the week. Next week you can try choosing your own spot again."

△

Mrs. Pike masterfully administers natural consequences while maintaining positive relationships with her students in a way that helps her young students understand proper behavior and their role in managing themselves. Having high expectations does not mean turning into a drill sergeant. Quite the contrary; when we apply natural consequences with compassion and empathy, students will comply and internalize the expectations. Using fear and intimidation are always counter-productive because students see us, rather than their own behavior, as the source of aggravation. If we respond abrasively, students may never see the need to change their behavior because in the student's mind we are the issue (Faye and Funk, 1995).

Having high expectations for our students requires that we provide clear expectations. As a teacher I always handed out the unit test on the first day that we started a new unit. I had a "begin with the end in mind" (Covey, 1989) strategy. Typically, this consisted of one side of one piece of paper with all of the questions listed by topic.

For a history test, the topics might include people and places, terms, short answer questions, and essay questions. For geography, the questions were divided along the five themes of geography. We began each unit by first going over the test which was the primary basis for their evaluation. We looked at each section and as we discussed what was there, I was able to discern which areas the students seemed to have more understanding in than others, which helped inform my teaching. As we progressed through the unit we would review the questions regularly to check for understanding. There was no mystery as to how the students were going to be evaluated. Students sometimes feel like they "have to read the teacher's mind to figure out what is going to be on the test." I was criticized by colleagues for this practice because I was "teaching to the test." If we aren't teaching to the test, then to what are we teaching? If we are studying the Civil War, the test should not include quadratic equations. Because nothing was hidden, I could expect every student to get an A, which was my goal.

Trusting students with responsibility is a tangible way to expect the best. Most students thrive on a challenge when we are willing to take the chance. Jim, a language arts teacher, talks about taking the leap with the school newspaper.

> The tough part of that is standing back and letting them do it. I can remember when I was first advisor to the newspaper. I spent a lot of Sunday nights putting together a newspaper and typing articles because they weren't doing it, whether it was due to laziness or whatever. As I got into it I decided, hey it's not my paper. It's one thing when you give them a title or a position. It's another to give them the responsibility; to stand back and watch them fail or succeed on their own and be their advisor rather than the doer. Everything is difficult the first time you try it but you just keep working at it. In time it eventually became a true student newspaper, not Jim's newspaper.

Jim's situation is especially tough because the publication's quality or lack thereof is representative of the program and the school.

Unlike a student term paper, the school newspaper is designed for public consumption and critique. Jim's leap of faith showed that he expected the best from his students while giving them an authentic publication experience.

Turning students into teachers requires guidance but is a wonderful way to raise the bar by saying to students, "You are the teacher, you are in charge of your education." Setting the parameters and expectations is a work in progress, until you develop the system that works best for you. You will encounter varying responses from students, ranging from eagerness to direct their own education and relishing the opportunity to be a classroom leader to apathy or rebellion from students for whom "sit and get" has become the comfortably preferable option. An obstacle for some students may be fear: fear of failure, fear of criticism, or simply the fear of being in front of a group. We can assist students in overcoming fear by welcoming mistakes as a natural part of learning, and modeling that failure is a temporary state of being, not the destination. There will be a learning curve for both you and your students, but in the long run the results will be outstanding. I am always impressed by the ingenuity our students demonstrate when given the opportunity to teach. If you already do this regularly, then I am preaching to the choir. If not, it may require a leap of faith, go ahead and jump!

While expecting the best is good educational practice and loving behavior, expecting perfection is neither. Expecting perfection sets everyone up for failure, including ourselves. Most accomplishments include some level of failure along the way. School is a testing ground for life, where we expect the best with the understanding that we don't always realize our hopes. Therefore, it is vitally important that we teach that failure is a temporary state which we overcome by starting over more intelligently and that all setbacks are amenable to hard work and persistence. No one is successful all the time. The greatest baseball players in the world fail to hit the ball safely about seventy percent of the time while the best three-point shooters in the NBA miss sixty percent of the time. Brett Favre has thrown more touchdowns than any quarterback in NFL history, but he also threw the most interceptions. Failure is an event, not a destination. As Peggy, a master teacher observed, "Children who experience unconditional love seem to be more willing to try new things because they feel no threat to being right or wrong. These children love being in school, love their teacher and would do anything to please them." We need to expect the best from each student, but expecting perfection is to seek what can't be achieved.

COACH ANDRIST

"Character cannot be developed in ease and quiet. Only through the experience of trial and suffering can the soul be strengthened, vision cleared, ambition inspired, and success achieved."

~ Helen Keller

Coach Andrist was a real model who expected the best of himself; therefore, he could reasonably expect the best from me. These two attributes are inexorably linked. There is an upward spiral associated with high expectations just as there is a downward spiral related to low expectations. High expectations have a way of self-reinforcing, leading to ever higher levels of achievement. When Coach gave his best I got better. The better I got the more I expected of myself.

Because he always stressed that the team took precedence over individual interests, Coach Andrist had high expectations of me as a team leader. Coach was famous for saying, "Anyone can be replaced," and he meant it. I was told many times, "Nolan, you can be replaced."

As a sophomore I became the first wrestler from my hometown to qualify for the state tournament. Although I lost my first two matches at the tournament, I was pleased with the accomplishment, too pleased, as things turned out. As a junior I was selected as team captain but my lack of maturity, being too full of myself, prevented me from adequately fulfilling the responsibilities of this position. While I won a lot of matches, I did not act like a captain in supporting and encouraging my teammates. I was in it for myself and it showed.

Each Monday after a tournament, Coach Andrist would talk about what we did well and what we were going to work on that week in order to get better. On this occasion he announced that I was going to be replaced as the team captain. He went on to tell the team how I was not fulfilling my responsibilities and why another teammate was better suited for that position. Of course he was right, and I learned that indeed I could be replaced. That was a painful but valuable lesson for me.

After practice Coach called me into his office and talked to me about the potential he saw in me as a leader and the things I needed to do to earn back the position of captain. He still believed in me, but he wanted to see if I could overcome my self-centered attitude to be worthy of being team captain. Just being good at something does not make you a leader. Certainly a leader needs to work for his own success, but he also has the responsibility of bringing others along in order to strengthen the team.

High expectations may include a wakeup call. The message Coach gave me was not a pleasant pill to swallow, but it was the truth. He gave it out of love for me as well as the team. When I got better as a leader the team got better.

Twice in my professional career I lost my job due to RIF, a Reduction in Force, where the staff members with the least seniority are let go due to budget constraints. Today the more common term is downsizing. Because I had learned that "I could be replaced," I never let losing my job bother me, and I always ended up in a better position on the other side. I thank Coach Andrist for teaching me that lesson as well as how to respond when you do get replaced.

My good friend Steve Baitinger reminded me of another story about Coach that all his wrestlers would remember. As we got closer to tournament time we focused on conditioning, which included ending practice with wind sprints. Vince Lombardi is famous for saying, "Fatigue makes cowards of us all," which it surely does. As we began to fatigue, the seduction of loafing through a sprint or two began to prey on our minds. When Coach sensed our reluctance to give our best effort he would say, "If you quit now you're going to quit in life." Years later Steve shared with me, "I didn't know what the hell he was talking about back then, but now I do." Coach Andrist used wrestling as the vehicle to teach about life. High expectations in performance, leadership, and work ethic were all part of the bargain.

Avoid Indifference

"The opposite of love is not hate, it's indifference. The opposite of art is not ugliness, its indifference. The opposite of faith is not heresy, it's indifference. And the opposite of life is not death, it's indifference."

~ Elie Wiesel

As mentioned earlier, according to a survey of nearly 150,000 sixth to twelfth grade students in 202 communities across the country, only 29% indicated they experienced a caring school climate (Scales and Leffert, 2004). The biggest complaint by students about teachers is that teachers do not seem to care (Noddings, 1992). Combine these numbers with the fact that a student drops out of school every 26 seconds—over a million students per year—and one could conclude that we have an epidemic of indifference. I submit to you that all of these numbers would dramatically improve if students believed that just one adult cared enough about their development and success to expect their best every day. Rigor is not a problem in our schools, boredom is; and the boredom is rooted in low expectations.

The following comments come from high school students who have teachers who do not expect the best. Skyler suggested, "Some teachers just show up to school and just go through the motions without really caring what we do. It hurts mentally and emotionally because I feel like they have given up on me. I feel detached from the community."

Michael contends that, "They don't put interest into me as a person, but only interest into me as a member of a class. I'm not an individual, but just a head in the classroom that helps them get a pay check. If teachers don't push you, you may just give up and think 'I can never do this.'"

Valerie had a teacher who would "make fun of my goals, dreams, and ambitions. That made me lose hope for my dreams." And finally,

Kim remarked that some teachers, "have no expectations, they expect only the bare minimum. That makes me feel unimportant and makes me not care about my work or how I do in school."

Clearly students feel loved when we expect the best of them. Dismissing a student's ambitions, making fun of their goals, or expecting the bare minimums communicate indifference regarding our students' abilities and our disinterest in them as unique individuals. While students may complain that we expect too much, the greater complaint, and the greater loss, is when we communicate indifference by expecting too little.

A WORD OF ENCOURAGEMENT

"I am not a teacher, but an awakener."

~ Robert Frost

For too many students, succeeding in school isn't cool. Many seem to be held back by a culture that tells them that succeeding is a matter of chance, that they are not the masters of their destiny, that they are predestined to a life of mediocrity, or that standing out by succeeding is a form of elitism. The sad truth is that the herd can be troubled by individual success. Teachers who model and teach the attributes which lead to success inspire students to take the risks emblematic of a life fully lived. Adults who believe and have faith in them, who expect the best, promote achievement and a fulfilling life. This is especially true for students who have not experienced success in the school setting. Expecting the best of our students requires risk taking that may be scoffed at by fellow educators. Believe, have faith, and expect the best anyway. Mark Twain once wrote that "Critics are those who ride in after the battle and shoot the wounded." Bless and then ignore your critics on this count. Be a dreamer not a critic. Be a builder of human capacity not a slayer of the human spirit. As a dreamer you may be criticized and scoffed at; be a dreamer anyway. It is the dreamers who promote beauty, reveal truth, and equip students to pursue the lives and dreams they have imagined. Dreamers always expect the best.

"If you think that compassion implies softness there's no way I can describe compassion to you, absolutely no way, because compassion can be very hard."

~ Anthony de Mello

Chapter Six:
Meet Students Where They Are

WHY MEETING STUDENTS WHERE THEY ARE IS LOVE AND WHY IT MATTERS

"When true love enters, you no longer like or even dislike people in the ordinary sense. You see them clearly and respond accurately."

~ Anthony de Mello

Meeting students where they are involves the total acceptance and unconditional positive regard for each student as an individual possessing unique gifts and aspirations, while rejoicing in their distinctive nature as free, growing, and sacred members of the human family. Our awareness of each student's social, emotional, and academic development equips us to respond to the needs of each student. Our unconditional acceptance of each student promotes self-acceptance and self-compassion by which each student is able to fully actualize their gifts. We embody love when we provide the freedom for each student to simply and completely be themselves.

Each student is a unique creation whose distinctive identity will never be repeated. From this perspective each student's life is deserving of awe and wonder. When we look at our students anew each day, they are allowed to be themselves and to mature and develop naturally without the crippling effect of judgment. A vital aspect of any education is self-discovery, applying the ancient Greek maxim: "Know thyself." Students can only know themselves when they are encouraged to be themselves. Acceptance also allows for the largest variety of distinctiveness in the classroom, reflecting the true diversity of the human condition.

Perhaps the most persistent challenge we face is educating each student in ways that respond to their unique nature. In a class of twenty-five students the range of interests, abilities, motivation, and efficacy is for all practical purposes infinite. Some students require a high level of academic support while others master the material in spite of anything we have to offer. For the latter our test is to challenge them in ways that are interesting and meaningful. For the former, regular interventions are required to meet their needs. The willingness and ability to "see them clearly and respond accurately" requires high levels of awareness and love. The root word for educate is educe, meaning to draw forth that which is latent or potential. Fundamentally our job is to draw forth the latent potential of each student, which requires a personalized approach. Accepting the unique character of each student is vital to assisting each student. When students experience acceptance, their natural curiosity and talents manifest themselves, they take more risks, respond to intuition, and see failure as a temporary setback rather than an inevitable destination. The following accounts illustrate how master teachers meet students where they are.

SAYING WHAT NEEDS TO BE SAID, BY SAYING NOTHING AT ALL

"Truly loving another means letting go of all expectations. It means full acceptance, even celebration of another's personhood."

~ William James

I was fortunate to spend a year teaching in beautiful Sitka, Alaska, which is located on the western edge of Baranof Island along Alaska's Inside Passage. In Sitka it rains a lot, about 150 inches per year, so sunny days are at a premium and reason for celebration.

Bald eagles are common in Sitka, with their numbers increasing every spring during the mating season. My classroom, and that of my colleague Paul, a math teacher, faced a hillside covered with beautiful Sitka spruce. Virtually the entire wall facing the hillside was made of glass windows. Because it rained so often, looking out the windows was usually not much of a draw, but on this spring day the sun was smiling on the hillside, summoning the eyes of Paul's students to linger in that direction. Adding to the verdant beauty were dozens of bald eagles perched in the trees. While seeing that many eagles was not unusual, the tranquility of the scene beckoned as this was one of the first sunny days we had experienced in a long while. Sitka winters tend to be long, dark, and rainy, so it was natural for the minds of students to wander when the first day of spring had arrived.

Paul was engaged in explaining some mathematical formula when he noticed that the entire class was equally engaged in looking at the eagles perched in the trees on this beautiful spring morning. We've all been there. We're doing our best to present an engaging lesson, but alas, we've lost them. Or, more accurately describing this episode, they had lost Paul. The mind floods with curt things one might say, designed to leave a minor wound while getting the attention of our charges back to the business at hand. After all, what could be more interesting than polynomial equations? But Paul, this loving teacher, took another tack; he met the students where they were.

Without missing a beat Paul strolled over to the window with his white board marker and continued the lesson, writing the equation on the window through which the students' gazes were fixed. The realization on the students' part was not immediate. After all there is an experience of transcendence when one is mesmerized by the magnificence of nature. But with patience on Paul's part, and the whispers of the students as they became aware of the situation, everyone understood Paul's intent. Once he had their attention Paul said, "It seems that this pen does not write on the window very well. I'm going to go back to the white board to continue. I invite you to join me there when you are ready." Appreciating both his method and his motive, all of the students eventually re-engaged with the lesson.

Paul reconnected each student to the lesson without wasting time, raising his voice, getting angry or antagonizing students who were understandably lost in the beauty of the moment. He met the students where they were, on a beautiful hillside in southeast Alaska, bringing them back to the world of advanced math.

HOMEWARD BOUND

"Don't take 'no' for an answer, never submit to failure."

~ Sir Winston Churchill

Meeting students where they are sometimes involves meeting them outside of school. Kris's story illustrates how he tried to meet one of his students where that student wasn't supposed to be during the school day: at home.

> I had a gang related student who was habitually truant from my class. He was an extremely bright kid but just had a hard time showing up. He was a Hmong kid and I think he struggled with the language barrier as well as the cultural differences. During my lunch on a day he was missing in class I went to his home. He was not there but I was able to talk to a number of his family members including his mom, dad, grandfather, and several aunts and uncles. I think I met the whole family. I was also able to speak with some of his neighbors as well. Apparently they gave him a bit of a talking to after he got home. He was in class the next day and every day after that for the rest of the semester. Our deal was he would come to class and I wouldn't go to his house looking for him. I think he got enough lectures from his family that he didn't need one from me.

One unannounced trip home by a concerned teacher made this student come to school every day. I have worked with several principals and counselors who regularly went to students' homes to pick them up to make sure they got to school. Some might correctly argue that this is enabling students or that students should be more responsible. But in these cases, just getting to school was the limiting step that prevented these students from realizing their potential. Once they got to school they were fine, in fact in most cases they flourished. In some cases, meeting students where they are requires meeting them at their own front doors. I salute the educators willing to go this extra mile. What a great way to say that failure is not an option, that I will meet you where you are, even at your home.

ALL ARE WELCOME

"The first thing a kindness deserves is acceptance, the second, transmission"

~ George MacDonald

High school coaches are sometimes viewed as ultra-competitive individuals who reserve their best coaching for the most gifted athletes. Pamela, a young teacher who played tennis competitively at the college level, shares a story about her high school tennis coach who excelled in supporting all of his student-athletes regardless of their ability.

> I have always admired my high school tennis coach because he didn't put the progress or the product of the program above the kids he was coaching. He showed that by opening the team up, so that we didn't have cuts. It was the only team in our school that had special education students on it who actually competed. None of them were on the varsity team but he would always arrange for them to have matches just like the rest of the team. Mostly none of them ever won but that didn't seem to matter to him. He would spend a lot of one-on-one time coaching them to get better. He didn't make other players feel badly at all because he didn't just focus on the varsity players. He shared his time equally with everyone. I always thought, Wow! This is kind of cool that we could have such a mixed team in that way. It was kind of a unique experience.

It can take courage to genuinely meet every student where they are, particularly in the highly charged arena of competitive athletics. Pamela appreciated being on a team where the coach genuinely accepted students regardless of their skills, while at the same time working to improve the play of each competitor. What a difference it would make if each of us adapted our classrooms so that every student was genuinely accepted for who they were and taught with the same passion regardless of their ability.

Relevance

"What is genius but the power of expressing a new individuality?"

~ Elizabeth Barrett Browning

John, a high school social studies teacher and baseball coach, discusses the challenge of addressing a wide variety of student interests and experiences while making the curriculum relevant.

> I have to work harder to include every little sub-group, because in teaching a subject like psychology it's very easy to have an example from the news or from athletics. But what about that guitar guy, how does it affect his world? And what about the guy who's into alternative music, or what about the girl who does dance? I don't know anything about dance but I have to try to find an example that fits that student's life. And by doing that I try to show that I am aware that there is more than just my perspective. They have different perspectives and athletics and the news is no more important than whatever it is that is different in that student's life. Being able to connect with all of my students' interests can really be challenging, but it is what brings relevance to them that counts.

In order to connect with students in what Glasser (1990, 1993) identifies as the student's "quality world," we may have to learn about a variety of topics including NASCAR, the World Wrestling

Federation, candle making, snowboarding, kayaking, or whatever interests our students. While many of these topics may not seem interesting on the surface, when you talk with students who are passionate about them it is easy to understand the attraction. Meeting students where they are is hard work, but the journey is worthwhile as it helps us discover the genius in every student.

WHAT TEACHERS AND STUDENTS SAY

"As we grow as unique persons, we learn to respect the uniqueness of others."

~ Robert H. Schuller

Karen Zich, a high school at-risk coordinator, shares her wisdom about why meeting students where they are emotionally is so important.

Each student is a unique and moldable individual, so caring and dealing with them should be done just as uniquely. The old adage, "different strokes for different folks" is a statement I hold to be true. It reminds me of a saying I heard another speaker use, "I will be fair with everyone, but I can't treat everyone equally." That statement made me realize this is what I do, even though I never thought of it in those terms. Treating everyone fairly means every child I come in contact with gets what he or she needs to be successful. However, the means and end result is going to be different for each child since I can't treat them all exactly the same. That would be defeating the purpose because what one child needs is different from the next child. This idea makes total sense and I use this method when working with students. I have found that explaining this concept to the students I work with helps them better understand me and my motives. In return, they're not so quick to say, "It's not fair."

A similar adage suggests, "There is nothing more unfair than the equal treatment of unequals." This concept recognizes the fact, confirmed by both the multiple intelligences (Gardner, 1993) and learning styles (Pritchard, 2009) research, that we all have gifts and deficits. As we personalize education it follows that we should let students know that we are individualizing responses because we see them as individuals who possess unique talents.

Dianne, a mid-school teacher, suggests a "tool" that may be the most important tool at our disposal in reading and meeting every student where they are.

> Through the years I have found that being a caring teacher is all about heart. A person's heart is a very smart tool. This tool can guide and help me see what it is a student needs at any given moment, be it a hug, a joke, a pat on the back, talk time with me, or a ten-minute timeout from work. I try to listen to my heart and do what I feel that individual child needs at that time. There are a lot more family and social issues that today's students are faced with, so having an advocate at school they can trust and go to with their worries is important to me. I have found that relying on the instinct of my heart is the most accurate measure I have to know when a student is in need of something. Sometimes we might have to stretch the rules a bit to let kids know teachers are human and have their best interest at heart. Being a teacher isn't all about rules and being the dictator of lectures and homework. It is also a work of the heart.

Great teachers seem to have a natural instinct regarding the needs of their students. I don't know if this type of skill can be developed through teacher training and experience, or if it is simply a gift. If you have this gift I encourage you to trust it and use it.

Adjusting our teaching in response to the wide range of knowledge and skills present in our classrooms is one of the biggest challenges we face. Mark shares his experience and practice as he takes his students through a test review. Answering questions in front of the class can be intimidating for many students. Mark offers some wisdom about promoting an environment where it is safe to "think out loud."

> I do say easy questions work when you're trying to address kids at their current level. Like when I do a review and I call on different little groups. And if one group is really faltering I'll save an easy question for them and then the others say, "Why do they get all the easy questions?" But then I say, "These are totally random," which they are not. Or when I have a kid like Joey in my class who gets every question right and I will save a tough one for that group. They will probably still get it right, but asking a kid a question if you are pretty sure they can answer it is a viable technique. I think it makes for a safe environment. It gives them that confidence to maybe sometimes try for harder things. They might think, "I know I got this one, maybe I can move on to something else."

When students feel vulnerable about their ability to perform in front of the class it inhibits responses (Tauber, 1998). Mark understands that gauging questions to each student's level is a way of building confidence and creating a safe environment. Another good technique to use is to state questions as invitations. "Would someone please explain the similarities between World War II and the Cold War?" Another teacher might use an introductory remark like, "This may be too difficult right now, but could someone please attempt to explain the connection between the Magna Carta and our Bill of Rights?" Inviting conjecture is a safe way to meet students where they are academically.

Non-directional questioning is another safe way to check for understanding while promoting critical thinking. Rather than asking Joey what he thinks about the national debt we might ask, "Joey, what might someone in France say about the impact of the $18 trillion national debt now carried by the United States government?" While on the one hand there is safety in speculating what someone else believes about a topic, we still gain insight as to the student's level of understanding. This may seem like sleight of hand; nevertheless, the non-directed nature makes it safe for Joey to answer virtually any question.

Students have very hectic schedules including school work, extra and co-curricular activities, jobs, caring for siblings, applying for college and scholarships, Boy Scouts, 4-H, and the list continues. Barbara describes how she personalizes education by meeting her students' time schedules:

> Deadlines are important but need to be flexible. I try to have an awareness of what's going on with my students, and the Madrigal group is a perfect example for me right now. I had a couple of girls not take the test today. They came in and asked, "Mrs. Johnson, are we taking the quiz today and then taking the test by the end of the week? Can we have ten or fifteen minutes to study for the quiz?" I told them, "Here's the quiz upside down. Get it to me by the end of the hour. You pick the time. If you need 35 minutes to study and 5 minutes to take it, that's fine, it's up to you. You decide and make it work."

Not only was Barbara aware of her students' needs, she empowered them within reasonable limits to solve the issue in their own time frame. Barbara sent a great message, not only in meeting the needs of her busy students, but in granting them the authority to address the issue in their own fashion.

Capitalizing on a student's natural talents is another way to personalize education. Mike describes the impact when Randy, a social studies teacher, encouraged a student to use his artistic talents to meet a history requirement.

> Harold was probably not the best history student. Memorization and writing were not his strong points. He was however, very creative and artistic, and he used his talents to do his history project in Randy's class. The final product was just outstanding and did show that he understood the concepts they were looking for. You could see the difference in how Harold responded not only to Randy but other teachers too. He felt really proud. He just felt like he had accomplished something and he held himself in high regard because other people, including his classmates, did as well. I will tell you he's a great student

now. I have him in government class. He got a B on his own. He worked really hard on getting everything in. I think the one thing that really got him to turn the corner was when Randy encouraged him to do that project. That was really in his comfort zone so he experienced some success and there has been no looking back for him. I think it was that type of thing that got him to work harder in his other classes. He felt good about who he was because he demonstrated some real strengths there.

The key here is that Randy allowed Harold to work in "his comfort zone." Competency in any subject can be demonstrated in a variety of ways. Because Randy understood Harold's strengths, he was equipped to be creative in matching Harold's natural gifts with the requirements of the history curriculum. When Harold experienced success in that context, a whole new world of achievement lay ahead for him. Because Randy met Harold where he was, he empowered Harold to continue his journey of self-discovery.

The research in both learning styles and multiple intelligences encourages us to capitalize on each student's natural gifts. When we start with the natural gifts that each student possesses we build on a solid foundation. Explicitly or implicitly, most students are aware of their gifts and hope that we teach them in ways that complement these talents. A student told me he is more successful when "teachers show me the way to success by conducting class in the way I learn best."

Offering choices and empowering students to direct significant aspects of their own education are other ways to meet students where they are. A graduate degree program is an excellent example of how well this can work. Having full authority to choose your own question and dissertation topic can be difficult, but it is also empowering and liberating. What is more meaningful than studying what interests us? We can do this on a small scale for younger children and expand the opportunities and responsibilities as students progress through school. Many schools now offer a senior project credit option based on this concept. I have personally seen students starting businesses, getting published in national magazines, doing extraordinary service projects, and creating outstanding works of art and technology through a senior project experience. Unleashing human potential is at the heart of our calling. Meeting students where they are is the place to start.

COACH ANDRIST

"Give love and unconditional acceptance to those you encounter, and notice what happens."

~ Wayne Dyer

Like all great coaches, Coach Andrist had the knack of getting the most out of the guys on our team despite the differences in abilities and temperaments. Each of us won a lot of matches, but we won in different ways. Neal was the cagy guy who did not have a lot of natural ability and could only do two or three moves well, but it worked for him. He got behind in nearly every match but won because Coach convinced him that he was never out of any match, and that if he was patient and waited for the right moment he could always pin his opponent. Jeff's gift was brute strength so Coach taught Jeff how to wear his opponents down and grind them into the mat. Jeff was not a great technician but won because of his strength and conditioning. Steve was slick, a great technician, who had mastered the duck under and double leg. Steve was great on his feet so he would take his opponent down, let him up, and take him down again, time after time. That was his path to success. Drew was the total enigma. Drew had no strength, quickness, or endurance, all of which are important assets of a successful wrestler. I have no idea how Coach got Drew to win any matches, but in his senior year he won over 20 matches and was the regional champion. He was so unorthodox that other wrestlers could not figure him out. This was by design of course, because Coach Andrist could help anybody figure out a way to win with the gifts they possessed. Coach developed whatever assets an athlete had into a winning formula by meeting each athlete where they were and accentuating their natural abilities. Coach didn't try to change anyone or wish that they could do things that did not fit their style. He just developed them into the best Neal, Jeff, Steve, and Drew possible. The classroom comparison is capitalizing on a student's natural learning style, intelligence, or interest. Any learning style can be an effective style.

Coach also met his athletes where they were emotionally. He knew which kids would respond to being chewed out and those who required more encouragement. Some were heavily invested in the sport and therefore could be pushed harder; for others their participation was more about social interaction and being on a team with friends than competing and winning. Coach accepted every student-athlete regardless of their innate abilities or motivation. By recognizing and accurately responding to each athlete's level of investment Coach made wrestling a winning experience for everyone, while at the same time developing champions.

Avoid Personal Convenience

"Whatever crushes individuality is despotism, by whatever name it may be called"

~ John Stuart Mills

We must be a stable influence in the lives of our students through modeling both interpersonal and intrapersonal intelligence (Armstrong, 1994). Interpersonal intelligence is the ability to see clearly and respond accurately to students' moods, desires, motivations, and temperaments. Intrapersonal intelligence involves self-knowledge and responding appropriately regardless of how we feel. We all have days when it is harder to perform than others, when personal issues make it difficult to be in a giving and accepting mindset. This does not, however, give us the right to disregard or subordinate student needs to our own personal convenience. We may have to adjust what we planned for the day, but students should never be victimized by stray voltage from our own worldly trials. If we begin a class by announcing, as one student reported, "I am having a bad day, you're just going to have to deal with it," it sends a clear message that the class is going to be run for the teacher's convenience and not for the benefit of the students. This despotic attitude will derail any attempt at teaching and learning. As the leaders in the classroom, we must rise above our self-centered tendencies. We have chosen to serve, not to be served. Our focus must always be on our students' needs and not our own personal convenience.

A WORD OF ENCOURAGEMENT

"It is dangerous to make everybody go forward by the same road: and worse to measure others by oneself."

~ St. Ignatius Loyola

Accepting students for who they are, without the illusion of what we think they should be, is simply accepting reality. When students feel accepted they don't have to put up a façade or struggle with trying to be someone or something they are not. They have the freedom to be themselves in all the beauty and wonder in which they were created. This includes the recognition that we all have fluctuations in our daily energy and how we perform. For instance, in your classroom you may notice that Larry is having a really good day but Doris didn't get much sleep last night, and something is clearly bothering Eric. Billy may need to work independently today because he doesn't seem to be working well with his group. Pat understands this material well so this is a great opportunity for him to be a leader. Virginia is clearly under the weather; she should probably take the test another day. Seeing our students anew each day allows us to meet the naturally fluctuating conditions and needs of our students.

There are many paths leading to the same destination. Some are harder, some take longer, and some turn out to be dead ends. We need to accept that each student is equipped to choose their own path in life. Acceptance does not require agreement. We don't have to agree with every action or point of view that our students hold. When students are clearly wrong, we have a responsibility to engage them in considering alternate perspectives. But we accept their right and responsibility to live as unique individuals who are doing their best to make their way in the world. The path chosen by some students, paraphrasing Thoreau, may be the one less traveled. For some that may make all the difference. If we accept students for who they are without expending the unnecessary energy to mold them into an image we prefer, we can focus on simply loving and supporting them on their journey of self-discovery.

"At the heart of personality is the need to feel a sense of being lovable without having to qualify for that acceptance."

~ Dr. Paul Tournier

PART III

Charismatic Connection

PART III
·················
Charismatic Connection

"Good teaching cannot be reduced to technique: good teaching comes from the identity and integrity of the teacher."

~ Parker J. Palmer

A charism is a gift shared with another. In this case the gift is ourselves. The charismatic connection is at the core of who we are as human beings, our essence. It involves personal qualities which are the source of our influence with students and which address the question of why students willingly do what we ask them to do. The charismatic connection manifests as a unique asset of leadership or worthiness which students are attracted to and willingly follow. It is never associated with fear or coercion, nor is it based on positional authority. It is more accurately described as principled authority which inspires confidence while inviting cooperation. Students willingly cooperate because of who we are as opposed to our positional authority as a teacher. The influence endures because students believe not only in what we are doing, but in who we are as human beings. A charismatic teacher is genuine, a real model, not a disingenuous role model telling students, "Do as I say, not as I do."

There are many approaches in education and psychology endorsed as effective ways to promote human development. Evidence suggests that in both fields the approach is largely incidental to promoting development while the agent of change, the human element, is the real key. Please consider the following passage and, after reading it, substitute "teacher" for "therapist" and consider whether you agree.

"The person of the therapist is the converting catalyst, not his order or credo, not his spatial location in the room, not his exquisitely chosen words or denominational silences. The dispensable trappings of dogma may determine what a therapist thinks he is doing, what he talks about when he talks about therapy, but the agent of change is who he is" (Lewis, Amini, and Lannon, 2000, p. 187). The charismatic connection addresses the "who we are" question which is the most important question asked by students. What we have to offer is important. Who we have to offer matters most.

The Saint

"In later life, as in earlier, only a few persons influence the formation of our character; the multitude pass us by like a distant army. One friend, one teacher, one beloved, one club, one dining table, one work table are the means by which one's notion and spirit of orientation affect the individual."

~ Jean Paul Richter

Mr. Michaels is a classic case of the charismatic connection; students are drawn to and influenced by him simply for who he is. He is also representative of the many teachers whose lives are an inspiration to students, even those they don't work with directly. The following conversation took place between several students who described the characteristics of this revered teacher and his life of service. They do not talk about his pedagogical mastery or infinite knowledge, nor do the classes he taught ever come up in the conversation. Their discussion focuses solely on who he was as a person, how he lived before his students, and how they responded to his beautiful example.

"I don't know how to describe Mr. Michaels. He is the most genuinely caring person; he cares so much. He would just come in and help us with volleyball. He used to be a volleyball coach so he came in and worked with us. It had nothing to do with how well we performed, we didn't win many matches, but he still came in. With all students he finds ways of pulling out their good traits and then working with that."

"Even if you aren't in any of his classes he still stops you and says 'hi.' He still knows everyone. I saw him at the mall the other day and he said 'hi.' He's just a genuinely nice person and seems to see the good in everyone."

"It was like the middle of last year he got Joe a job over across the street. Before that Joe had an attendance of like 5 percent. He was hardly ever at school. By the end of that year it was up to like 80 percent. He was going to work and coming to school, he was having a good time. He was a changed person because Mr. Michaels had taken an interest in him. He got his hair cut and he cleaned himself up. At the beginning of this year he started showing up for school all the time. He was working on bigger projects and then all of a sudden, boom, he started his own business. I would say 99 percent of that was all due to Mr. Michaels. He went out to his house and he was like there most days for over an hour and the kid was just showing him what he had done. He showed him lawn mowers that he built and motorcycles and chain saws he had restored. He went from doing nothing to having his own business in less than a year and he's going to graduate. I never would have thought that could happen."

"When a teacher puts so much time into each individual student that they have, like a friend of mine, I kind of grew up with the kid. I see this kid once in a while and she was supposed to have graduated last year. It's kind of sad to see how he puts all of his time into coming to school and then for like the past three years she's still here when she shouldn't be. He's the most respectful teacher. He's put all this time into Jill for three years and he is still trying to get her to come to school and graduate. He doesn't quit trying. He says 'I am not giving up on Jill.' She's supposed to graduate the past three years, she's still here, and she's going to be here until she's twenty-one and like he never gives up. His patience is unbelievable. It's amazing to think that a teacher cares that much. That a person cares that much—anybody!"

"You don't see that a lot these days. You'll see someone broken down on the highway and I don't know if this has much relevance, but most people would just drive past without giving it a second thought. He would be the kind of person that would stop and help him out. Not only help him out but take him and help him buy a tire if he didn't have the money. I think he'd do anything for anybody."

"This one girl I work with, she used to go to a different school and she would have to wait a year or two more to graduate. She wasn't going to do that. But if she drives here every day she'll graduate this year. He goes way out of his way. He finds a way to help them graduate. She didn't even go to our school but when he found out about her, he talked her into at least trying it here. I think she's going to make it."

"I've even heard like a student swearing at him and like he is just completely calm. He's not afraid to discipline them. He'll bend over backwards to help you but he's not going to let you get away with anything. He'll lay down the law."

Mr. Michaels embodies the three character traits which are the focus of this section: enthusiasm, empathy, and respect, and he exhibits these attributes genuinely. Genuineness may be the most important aspect of the charismatic connection because students will spot phony enthusiasm, empathy, and respect from a mile away.

This conversation also demonstrates the reciprocal nature of love. These students, some who had never had him in a class, spoke enthusiastically and with a high level of respect about how he understood and cared for his students, how he loved them. There are many character traits exhibited by loving teachers, traits that students respect, are drawn to, and admire, but enthusiasm, empathy, and respect have a universal appeal to students. These traits are returned to us by the students we serve. As you read the following chapters please consider how you communicate the very nature of your being: who you have to offer.

"…when focusing on talents, we tend to forget that our real gift is not so much what we can do, but who we are. The real question is not 'What can we offer each other?' but 'Who can we be for each other.'"

~ Henri J. W. Nouwen

Chapter Seven:
Enthusiasm

WHY ENTHUSIASM IS LOVE AND WHY
ENTHUSIASM MATTERS

"The person who loves becomes enthusiastic, filled with the sparkle and the joy of life. And then he goes on to fill it full of meaning."

~ Norman Vincent Peale

Enthusiasm is the outward expression of the love of life itself. As educators we enthusiastically say "yes" to exploration, creativity, ingenuity, and learning. Enthusiasm allows us to see all that life has to offer, while emphasizing the most meaningful aspects of our lives and compelling us to do what we love and love what we do.

Enthusiasm remains one of my favorite attributes in a teacher. The root word of enthusiasm, *entheos*, translates as "the god within." It is the characteristic that gives us the god-like power to inspire. The root word for inspire, *spirare*, means "to breathe life into." Truly, enthusiastic teachers breathe life into the educational experience for students. Our enthusiasm is infectious, making students look forward to coming to class and desiring more when they leave. Enthusiasm whets the appetite for learning, motivating students to have an open mind, engage in learning, and give their best.

As educators we are in the business of selling every day. As Norman Vincent Peale (1967) suggests, "enthusiasm persuades and persuasion sells" (p. 39). Each day it is our enthusiasm that sells the ideas that schooling is important, learning is exciting, and what we are offering is valuable. Without enthusiasm there is no sale, no learning and as one student remarked, learning becomes "a hateful chore." Enthusiasm is the aspect of love that ignites the imagination, providing meaning and purpose to each day's lesson. We are most influential when we are both intellectually and emotionally stimulating, inspiring our students to higher levels of commitment and achievement (Goleman, 1998).

YODA

"Nobody grows old merely by living a number of years. We grow old by deserting our ideals. Years may wrinkle the skin, but to give up enthusiasm wrinkles the soul."

~ Samuel Ullman

Dr. Simmons, my Minnesota history professor, embodied enthusiasm in his teaching. Initial impressions would not lead one to expect this, as Dr. Simmons was a frail, smallish, unassuming man, sort of a miniature Dumbledore without the dunce cap. As he teetered into the room you were never sure if he was going to make it to the podium; it seemed a mild gust of wind might blow him away. As he slowly took off his wraps (this is the only way to describe what he wore—I think he was born before coats were invented), he continued to shrink until there was nothing left but a poncho, skin and bones, and a huge white beard. Then it happened. As he began to teach his entire being came to life, and like Superman coming out of the phone booth ready to take on the world, he was transformed into a character from another time. His unbridled enthusiasm for teaching radiated for the next hour as he jumped on the table to demonstrate how voyageurs paddled their canoes and, beaming like a lighthouse, spun yarns of heroes, villains, sinners, and saints, making it seem as if these characters from our past were with us today. With nothing more than his own being he brought history to life right before our eyes. One could not help being engaged, mesmerized, inquisitive, and grateful to be in the presence of a man who had such a lust for life and the subject that he taught. In what seemed like a few minutes, the hour had passed. Dr. Simmons lived more enthusiastically in that hour than most people do in a month. As the students shuffled out of class he reapplied his layers of clothing, staggered to the door and was gone. His enthusiasm was a model and inspiration for anyone who wanted to teach history, as I did.

"LIFE! LIFE!"

"Enthusiasm is that secret and harmonious spirit which hovers over the production of genius."

~ Isaac Disraeli

Lowell Baltz holds the distinction of being the only teacher to give me an F for a grade. More accurately stated, his was the only class in which I earned an F. As a freshman I earned an A during the first grading period, and then inexplicably had a minor slump earning an F in the second nine-week grading period. I am convinced that during my freshman year my neo-cortex intermittently detached from the rest of my brain as extended spells of stupidity were definitely part of my ninth grade experience. There may be some other explanation, but this is the one I'm sticking with. I couldn't tell you any other grades from my high school years, but I distinctly recall each of my nine-week grades from my freshman earth science class (A-F-A-C) because of the comment Mr. Baltz made, with a look of wonder and awe, as he handed me my year-end report card. "Mr. Nolan, I hope you can explain this pattern...I sure can't." My explanation remains what many believe to be a common malady unique to the adolescent male, *neo-corticus intermittentess disconnectus*.

Sharing the study of life science made Mr. Baltz come alive, no pun intended. I vividly remember the day we were all looking through our microscopes witnessing asexual reproduction, where one cell splits into two. I thought it was interesting but, based on Mr. Baltz's reaction, you would have thought we were witnessing the Big Bang. He looked at me and my lab partner and asked, "Do you see it?" We said "yes." He looked at us with increased intensity, as if he were looking into the depth of our souls, the kind of look that makes you feel a little squeamish, and asked again, "Do you see it?" A little unnerved by the question and the look on his face, and wondering if indeed I did see "it," I haltingly said, "Umm…I think so." After peering into our microscope his eyes caught mine in a riveting gaze and he shouted, "Life!!! Life!!! You are witnessing the creation of new life!!!"

Initially he scared the dickens out of me, thinking maybe he had snapped. But as he glided from table to table peering into the microscopes he continued shouting, "Life! Life!" His enthusiasm gave me a greater appreciation for the study of biology. This level of animation was standard fare for Mr. Baltz; it was one of the traits that made him so endearing. He was absolutely giddy when we celebrated the first Earth Day in 1970 by building a student park outside the school. He absolutely loved what he did.

Mr. Baltz modeled a zest for life well beyond the schoolhouse doors. He lived with that same passion, spending summers planting trees for the Forest Service and joining the Peace Corps to teach natives in Belize to grow fish. All of these experiences no doubt enriched his life, but they also enriched the lives of those he served. Mr. Baltz truly has "the god within."

THE FART MACHINE

"I prefer the folly of enthusiasm to the indifference of wisdom."

~ Anatole France

The willingness to laugh, especially at ourselves, and appreciate the harmless humor of students, is an expression of enthusiasm. Frank, a high school science teacher, shares a couple of episodes that at first glance may seem a little uncomfortable, but left him and his students in stitches.

I've learned that it's important to laugh at students' jokes as long as they are clean. But yet their antics too, kids can be really funny. A couple of years ago there was a student in front of the class and he would kind of lean over and you'd hear this noise from him like he was passing gas. At first I just ignored it but a minute or so later he did it again and it was really loud. So I said, "Kevin, would you knock it off." He's sitting right next to this junior girl at the time, a very proper girl, and she's kind of moving farther away, and he did it again so I told him he needed to go out in the hallway. Then he starts laughing. Well, he and a buddy were using a remote controlled fart noise maker. He had it in his back pocket and there was somebody on the other side of the room hitting the button. It was so funny! I laughed for fifteen minutes at that. The whole class was just lost. Then I found out they did that to a chemistry teacher later that week. They put it in his desk. It was genuinely funny. If you can at least have the flexibility to enjoy some of their humor sometimes. It's important to appreciate their antics and remember they are kids. When you have the ability to be flexible it's best just to enjoy it.

It is moments like these that show our humanness. Frank could have chosen to make this a federal case, kicked the kids out of class or even involved the principal, but Frank chose otherwise. No one was harmed or belittled by this prank, and everyone seemed to get a kick out of it. To react otherwise would have made Frank seem less human, less joyful, less accepting of trifling behavior. Humor is an expression of enthusiasm at its highest level and is always appreciated by students. Laughter is also a bonding experience that can contribute to developing a more cohesive class structure. When the laughter is harmless and in good fun, just join in.

PRESS THE FLESH

"Love enables the person to treat life as an art which the person, as artist, is continually seeking to improve and beautify in all its aspects."

~ Ashley Montagu

Carl had grown weary of fighting the little battles that frequently occur in school; he had tired of walking the halls and having to correct students on their language, behavior, and the dreaded public displays of affection. He wished for a cloaking device that would allow him to travel the hallways in anonymity. Instead, Carl chose to enthusiastically embrace meeting each student with a friendly greeting and handshake as a means of overcoming his dread.

> Last year I just hated walking in the hallways because I always felt like I had to correct things. I had to pass seniors, juniors and sophomores just to get to the teachers' lounge. It was like a battle because I always had to say "quit doing this" or "quit doing that," and this year, man it is just so different—I like it!
>
> The one thing that I did was stand in front of my door each day and shake each kid's hand as they came into class. It's something that I thought would be a nice way to start each day and to maybe just make somebody's day. At first some kids thought it was corny but they seem to have grown to expect it and even like it. Now when I walk through the hallways it seems like the seas almost part and there are kids who I don't even have in class who want to shake my hand. I thought that was the coolest thing in the whole wide world. Sometimes my arms are full, I'm carrying books or something and a kid will still want to shake my hand. I think they might be making it a bit of a game, trying to catch me off guard, but that's alright. It's kind of cool for me. I don't hate walking in the hallways anymore.

Psychologist William James suggests that if we want something, as Carl did in this example, we can begin by acting as if we already have it. Carl wanted to feel comfortable in the halls again. His action—shaking hands with students as they entered his class—was the "as if" action that made the rest of his hallway excursions a pleasure. Carl enthusiastically embraced a solution to a situation he dreaded, acting "as if" he enjoyed it while creating a new reality. Like an artist he did something to beautify the situation for everyone involved and that beauty returned to him. When he changed the way he looked at his situation, the situation he looked at changed. Enthusiasm can seem corny, as it was to some of Carl's students—be enthusiastic anyway. Most students will appreciate you for it, and like other good infections it will spread; enthusiasm is contagious.

POLAR OPPOSITES

"People are about as happy as they make up their minds to be."

~ Abraham Lincoln

Enthusiasm is a choice requiring a high level of self-discipline. Many of the teachers I interviewed referred to the "self-talk" they engage in on days when they were not enthused about coming to school. One of the reasons I moved from teaching to administration after fifteen years was that I did not want to become a boring, disgruntled teacher who had lost the fire, after covering the checks and balances system of American government for the five-hundredth time. I sensed that if I did not make a change I was going to become that teacher.

I discovered that as an administrator I can still be a teacher but with a different message for a different audience. I too engage in "self-talk" because I know that if I am not excited about what I am sharing, the audience—usually the teaching staff—won't be either. In the following story, Amanda, a student, shares her experience with two teachers, one who was always pleasant and enthusiastic while the other was held hostage by his moods, seemingly oblivious to the freedom he possessed to choose his attitude.

I know one of my most positive teachers has to be Ms. Palmer. Every day she would come in with a smile on her face. There was not a day that she would have a bad mood because she thinks that if she is happier, it will make the class happier. She was just always a positive person, never said anything bad to anyone, and made all the negative things go away. It does make the class friendlier and happier having her be in a good mood. Like if she is happy, everybody else is and it makes everything else a lot easier because there is no tension or stress. And she is just so funny.

There is a difference between that class and math class. Because in her class you can joke around, she'll joke with you, crack jokes, make fun of the things she's teaching about and then that makes me remember it because she made it into a joke. It just makes it more fun. It's not boring. She gets you involved because you're not just sitting there getting lectured. In math class Mr. Peavey has come into class saying, "Okay, I'm having a bad day today so just deal with me." And it makes everyone else feel more tense because we've got to watch what we're doing. It really just makes the class harder to get through.

What a contrast. Ms. Palmer works hard to embody the atmosphere she knows is good for learning, while Mr. Peavey is stuck on himself and plainly states that it is the students' responsibility to adjust to his foul mood. Enthusiasm is a choice that has a profound effect on how well we perform and whether students engage in or withdraw from learning.

GIANTS OF THE EARTH

*"This is why I studied literature in college. This is why I became
a teacher: to share in grand conversations about books, to spread
the joy, to initiate and welcome students into the fraternity, into...
the 'club of clubs', to travel with them into wondrously familiar or
incredibly strange imaginative worlds."*

~ Jeffrey D. Wilhelm

Enthusiasm makes all that we experience delightful and meaningful. Darlene shares an enduring experience she had with a teacher
whose enthusiasm directed Darlene to her calling as an educator.

> I just loved my junior high school English teacher. I was
> in his class every day and I couldn't wait to get there. I
> thought, he's going to tell a story, we're going to be reading.
> I mean, *Giants of the Earth* is the most tedious Norwegian
> across the Dakotas book, but we loved it! And he had this
> way of talking to us and rocking back and forth on his feet
> and there were such great dynamics going on in the class.
>
> I remember when I was sitting there one day and he sat
> down beside me and said, "Stop and talk. What do you
> think is going on?" He asked my opinion. He said, "What
> do you think?" I never had a teacher ask me that before.
> And so I told him. And that's why I decided to teach
> English. That's when I fell in love with books and that
> whole classroom demeanor. Even when I started teaching,
> you know, you get some of those new teacher ticks, and I
> would call him and sob and he would write me letters. I
> would call him once a week just to visit. It's like I never left
> that class. The laughter is still there, the mannerisms are
> there and we talk about stuff that just makes it so good. If
> I could be a tenth of the teacher that he was I would be
> happy.

Darlene is carrying on the good infection about literature to
her own students. In her description we can readily sense that the
connection began with the person of her English teacher and who

he had to offer, the charismatic connection. It is that connection that helps students feel, "I never left that class."

What Teachers and Students Say

*"Learning should be a joy and full of excitement.
It is life's greatest adventure; it is an illustrated excursion
into the minds of the noble and the learned."*

~ Taylor Caldwell

Our enthusiasm directly impacts how students experience school and learning. As high school student Jamie described it, "They (teachers) are hyper in the morning. And they are like, 'This is the best time of day for us, la la.' Even though we're teenagers and we hate the mornings, we're happy." Infectious enthusiasm demonstrates a love of life and the unbridled joy we have as educators to be doing what we love and loving what we do. Enthusiasm for the sheer joy of learning is one of the most valuable models we offer our students.

Tammy appreciates enthusiastic teachers because "They're really passionate about what they teach and what they talk about. Like you can tell even after like ten years of doing the same thing they still enjoy it. It might be boring but they're all peppy about it." Peppy? What a wonderful compliment to be described as "peppy" about our teaching.

John, a high school teacher, describes the attributes of a fellow teacher he works with and admires.

> He is the greatest guy in the world. He works over at one of the middle schools. I had the opportunity to do two months of an assistant principal internship over there last year. The energy in his classroom, getting every kid to talk every day, surrounded by kids in the hallway, pumping them up, praising them, and calling them to task. How one person can give that much of himself in a day, every day, and never seem to tire is just amazing. I have never seen that much enthusiasm from one guy. He would never say no to anyone, student or teacher. He truly believes in

helping other people and the kids knew that. He is just tremendously selfless and motivating. He is a model for me.

I wonder if I could demonstrate that same level of enthusiasm and commitment every day. What if every one of us could? What a difference that would make in our schools. The really good news is that we can choose our attitude: choose enthusiasm at every moment.

Our enthusiasm can be expressed through the physical environment we create in our schools and classrooms. I always enjoy walking through elementary schools where student art work and other projects are displayed in the hallways because displaying student work is an expression of our enthusiasm for their accomplishments. Kim, an elementary teacher, describes how she sets up her classroom to promote enthusiastic behavior in her students.

> I believe the environment sets the stage for a warm, inviting, positive school attitude and enthusiastic behaviors. The more exciting the room the more they'll want to be there and explore. I create multi-faceted centers and free choice activities that are relevant to things that not only interest the children but also meet my teaching goals. The furniture is important. If the chairs, tables, and materials are child size they know it's special for them. Exploratory centers are relevant; a sandbox, water-table, puzzles, arts and crafts, great books, music and dramatic play centers are all part of the mix.

Peter, a high school psychology teacher, highlights a good sense of humor as promoting an enthusiastic classroom.

> Teachers communicate enthusiasm by having a sense of humor with students. It makes them feel more at ease and excited about what I am teaching. It makes them feel that you care enough to connect with them on a level that makes them comfortable. Something as simple as smiling goes a long way too. It's also important to appreciate the silly jokes they have. I was handing out a term sheet today and I had like twenty pink ones and thirty of that salmon color and I said to take whichever one you want. The first kid took a pink one—a big football player—and I

was like, "Well, Joe, that's good that you are comfortable with your masculinity." And he said, "Yeah, I feel pretty good about myself." I like that. We have accomplished our mission in psychology. It was a good joke that put everyone at ease.

Fun activities that connect students with rigorous academic work are another way to ignite the imagination. Jill, a high school student, provides several examples that helped her connect with the curriculum.

> I really get a lot out of my American history class when we play current events. The game is fun and my teacher always takes some time to show how what is going on today applies to the unit in history that we are studying. In my English class with Ms. Kimmerly we play Catch Phrase sometimes to help build our vocabulary. In science we do fun experiments on Fridays like blowing bubbles and lighting them on fire. Last year in chemistry we made ice cream using liquid nitrogen and then we got to eat it.

I don't know about you, but I never got to eat ice cream in my chemistry class. What a great way to illustrate chemical reactions and then have a little prize at the end. Ice cream would have spurred my enthusiasm for chemistry.

Carmon, a high school student, sums up this section with this insight: "A lot of teachers at this school seem to like what they teach. If the teacher likes his or her class, then the class is more fun for us because we have an enthusiasm for it because they do." Enthusiasm is about loving what we do. When we enthusiastically share our love for our subject and for learning, students are eager to get on board.

Each day we have a choice to approach our work with enthusiasm or indifference. We can start with gratitude for the opportunities we have. Henry David Thoreau used to begin each day lying in bed and identifying all the good things in his life: the good people, opportunities, and circumstances he experienced each day. This practice of counting our blessings is one way to feed our enthusiasm for our profession and all the different roles we play in life. It's easy to be enthusiastic when we realize how much we are blessed.

COACH ANDRIST

*"Enthusiasm releases the drive to carry you over obstacles
and adds significance to all you do."*

~ Norman Vincent Peale

Coach Andrist taught us that challenges were life's greatest gifts. Tough opponents and big tournaments were viewed as challenges to be treasured, not events to be feared. The biggest rivalries, whether we won or lost, were the most meaningful because we learned where we were along the path to realizing our full potential. Both victory and defeat offered opportunities to rejoice, lament, learn, and grow. The most challenging experiences were the most significant because they pushed us beyond what we believed to be our limits, allowing us to discover who we really were.

Coach's enthusiasm for life went beyond wrestling. One of his favorite leisure activities was digging ginseng. Coach took me on several ginseng digging expeditions where I saw a completely different side of him. We wandered the woods looking for the elusive root which I never was very good at finding. The peace of the woods was the most important part of the experience. Coach was always at peace, reflective and alive in the presence of nature. We would go long stretches without ever speaking and when we did, it was never about wrestling. Our conversations focused on life and dreams. There was a quiet enthusiasm and reverence for the natural world which he enjoyed immensely.

Coach Andrist was a great model for what it means to live a well-rounded life. Avocations bring joy, serenity, and significance to every aspect of our lives. While walking the Wisconsin woods back in the early 1970s Coach could never have imagined his current life raising thoroughbreds in Arizona. Enthusiasm for all that life offers carries us down roads never imagined. Coach continues to model for me what it is to be alive, to learn, to grow, buoyed by enthusiasm, down every trail he travels.

AVOID APATHY

"Science may have found a cure for most evils, but it has found no remedy for the worst of them all—the apathy of human beings."

~ Helen Keller

We can risk getting too comfortable in a particular teaching position and then, almost imperceptibly, losing enthusiasm for that assignment and falling into the complacency of comfort. It's like a quiet burnout, eluding our awareness. Comments like, "I can only teach third grade," or "I'm just a history teacher, I don't want to teach geography," or my least favorite, "I only teach AP and Honors courses," are examples of how we sometimes argue for our own limitations. Let someone else argue for your limitations; you have too much to offer to become complacent.

There is nothing wrong with teaching in our area of strength and interest; however, as educators we should constantly expand both. During my career I was blessed to teach physical education, American history, world history, America at war, psychology, sociology, Native American history, geography, government, street law, civics, economics, current events, and world religions and philosophies in grades 7 through 12. I also had the opportunity to coach football, baseball, basketball (having never played basketball, that was a real treat!), wrestling and hockey. With all of these different assignments, growth and adjustment were a constant. We expect students to progress and master different grade levels and subjects; shouldn't we do the same? Different responsibilities allow us to grow and appreciate the challenges characteristic of different grade levels and subject areas. Variety is the antidote to apathy.

Mandy was a great model for me and many other educators. To renew her enthusiasm Mandy chose to radically alter her teaching assignment every five or six years. She was very candid about why she chose this path when she told me, "Gerry, I'm getting stale. I need a new challenge or I'm going to end up being a burned out grouch."

Mandy started as a lower elementary teacher but through the course of her career taught high school special education, fifth grade, elementary special education, music, and high school at-risk students, before finishing her career working with mid-school at-risk students. Think how valuable this breadth of experience was for her professional growth. By seeking a broad range of assignments Mandy insulated herself from stagnation. If you are feeling stale in your own professional journey, make the jump to a completely different teaching assignment and experience how the juices start to flow anew.

Another form of apathy involves the intellectual laziness associated with labeling our students. Labels are easy; we accept them without considering their accuracy or how they institute limits for our students while masking their genuine abilities. Labels tell us nothing about their interests or talents. Labels do more to say "no" to an education than saying "yes." Once a student is labeled they become somebody else's problem. Too often regular classroom teachers use a student's label as an excuse to wash their hands of responsibility for that student.

My least favorite label is "Gifted and Talented." What does that mean? Gifted at what? Don't we believe every student is "Gifted and Talented" in some area? Are there only certain disciplines that rise to the level of including the label "Gifted and Talented?" I grew up down the road from Bruce Haire, who, before he entered high school, could take a car engine completely apart and rebuild it so that it ran better than when he started. Isn't that a gift? Today Bruce and the gift he had for mechanical work would never be recognized as "Gifted and Talented." I have often wondered if the valedictorian in our graduating class could have done what Bruce could do. And yet Bruce was one of the first students who went into special education classes when they started in our schools. Labels tell us next to nothing about a student, and obscure our view of the gifts and talents they possess.

You read about Tim in an earlier section of the book. He was identified by a fellow colleague as "not worth your time." Had Gary and others accepted this label, Tim would have never realized his potential academically or athletically. We have all heard the labels, "that class is nothing but trouble," "he's lazy," "she's a know-it-all," fill in the blank. Teachers sometimes even make medical diagnoses like "he's ADD," or "she's obsessive-compulsive." Let's leave the labels on the sidelines and the medical diagnoses to the medical professionals.

Commit to being students of your students, being aware of who they really are, and understanding their story despite the misleading labels employed in gossip and lounge talk. Whenever a label is applied to a student, be it good or bad, we have insufficiently defined them. While a student may appreciate being labeled as a "jock," "techie," "preppie," or any other term, it is self-evident that they are much more than the label suggests. Let's continue to do the hard work of seeing students anew each day and continuing to be optimistic about their potential for nearly unlimited growth. Labels are a sign of intellectual laziness, leading to apathy and excuses.

A WORD OF ENCOURAGEMENT

"Enthusiasm is the genius of sincerity and truth accomplishes no victories without it."

~ Edward G. Bulwer-Lytton

While your enthusiasm for teaching may be ridiculed by some, be confident that it enhances your effectiveness and is greatly appreciated by your students. Some will identify your joy as foolishness or unprofessional behavior (see fart machine); be joyous anyway. Just as we hope that students will define themselves through a healthy self-concept, your enthusiasm should define your approach to your work: that you love what you do. Be bold in modeling a ravenous appetite for the joy of living and learning. Wear your enthusiasm as a badge of honor for our profession. Boredom may be the greatest enemy in America's classrooms today. Enthusiasm is the antidote to boredom, breathing life into the imagination of every student we serve.

"A teacher who is attempting to teach without inspiring the pupil with a desire to learn is hammering on a cold iron."

~ Horace Mann

Chapter Eight:
Empathy

WHY EMPATHY STIMULATES LOVE
AND WHY IT MATTERS

"It is quite clear that between love and understanding there is a very close link...He who loves understands, and he who understands loves. One who feels understood feels loved, and one who feels loved feels sure of being understood."

~ Paul Tournier

The need to be understood is one of the great longings of the human spirit. Understanding, having empathy for our students, and accurately responding to their unique circumstances is love in action. Empathic love is the ability to feel or understand another person's internal state while at the same time exhibiting the ability to communicate our understanding to another (Rogers, 1983). Through empathy we experience our students' struggles so that we can help them navigate through issues in the hope that we can lighten their burdens.

Just as we are naturally wired to give and receive love, we are naturally wired to empathize. In the brain's anterior cingulate cortex, just behind the frontal lobes, are "pain neurons" which fire when we experience pain or when we witness the pain of others. However, just because we can feel another person's suffering does not mean we will respond in a meaningful way. While empathy is a feeling, love involves action. Empathy is the gateway to loving action, acting as a catalyst to bring forth our loving response to the distress that others are experiencing (Trout, 1999).

Teacher empathy given freely, particularly during the early stages of the relationship, is a predictor of future student success. Nonjudgmental empathy dissolves alienation while promoting a constructive student-teacher relationship. Through empathy we demonstrate an acceptance of the inherent value of each student which results in students developing more positive attitudes toward themselves and schooling (Rogers, 1980).

A variety of studies indicate that teacher empathy is correlated with higher student achievement. In a study of secondary school students, a positive relationship between empathy indicators and grade point average was observed (Bonner and Aspy, 1984). Schools in which students were involved in programs designed to increase empathy and create "caring communities" have higher scores than comparison schools on measures of higher order reading comprehension (Kohn, 1991). Correlations reflecting a positive relationship between empathy and school achievement are supported in the findings of experimental studies in which empathy training resulted in heightened achievement (Feshbach and Konrad, 2001). These and other studies suggest that empathy matters when our goal is improved academic performance.

Familiarity promotes empathy. This may explain our nearly exclusive concern for those who are physically and psychologically close to us, those whom Sorokin (1954) identifies as the "in-group." We tend to help and feel more responsible for those we know and who are like us because our common experience decreases the social distance between us (Trout, 1999). A broader sense of empathic love allows us to see all who are in need as equally deserving our love. Most teachers were good students so we tend to identify well with, and subsequently empathize with, successful students. The challenge of empathizing with those who are not successful students, whose experience is different from our own, is common. Bridging this gap is a function of empathic love.

THE CAGED ANIMAL

"You don't have to accept the invitation to get angry. Instead, practice forgiveness, empathy and encouragement."

~ Dan Fallon

We all have students for whom sitting still at a desk is not in their constitution. High energy is a gift that in some classroom settings can be problematic. Expecting these students to sit still for extended periods is folly; it is a rebellion against their nature. One of these students stands out in my teaching experience and thankfully we came to an arrangement that was mutually satisfactory.

Cameron was like a caged animal, but only in the physiological sense. Cameron had more energy than a Saturn rocket but he was also studious, engaging, insightful, inquisitive, and overall a wonderful student and a great asset to his classmates. The reality, however, was that Cameron just could not sit still. It wasn't that he did not want to sit still; he could not sit still. Physiologically, Cameron was hardwired for motion so expecting him to sit quietly in his desk for an extended period of time was like expecting a new born colt not to run.

We worked out a deal that Cameron could get up anytime, go to the back of the room and stand, walk, prowl, or do anything, as long as he did not interrupt the flow of the class. Occasionally I would make eye contact with Cameron which was our signal for him to go to the back and get moving. Cameron was respectful of his responsibilities with this arrangement because I was respectful of his needs. Other students took to doing the same thing under the same rules. This was a natural intervention because I could empathize with Cameron's genetically encoded nature. Research now suggests that an active body plays a key role in developing a sharp mind (Ratey, 2008).

"GET OUT OF MY CLASS."

"The only kind of dignity which is genuine is that which is not diminished by the indifference of others."

~ Dag Hammarskjold

It is interesting to note how differently two people can respond to an identical situation. I was three weeks late for my first semester of college with an excused absence. The dean of the college sent a letter to all my professors describing why I was late and when they could expect me in class.

Teacher empathy indeed is a predictor of future success. I strolled across the green to my first college class, English 101, on a mild and sunny September morning. Because I was three weeks late, I arrived to class early so that I could speak with the professor before class started. The class was conducted in "the pit," a large auditorium-like room with stadium seating for several hundred students. The sheer size of the room and all the people made me feel small. More people could fit in that auditorium than attended my high school. When I identified the teacher, I walked up to him smiling and introduced myself. He looked up from some papers he was shuffling, stared at me over the top of his reading glasses, and said, "Get out of my class." He knew who I was; he knew why I was late, and that my absence had been approved by the dean, but he insisted it was too late for any student to be joining his class. When I mentioned the letter from the dean describing my situation he shook his head, rolled his eyes, and made some inaudible remark. As I tried to explain further, he became hostile. He ripped his glasses from his head, pointed to the door, and said in a loud voice for everyone to hear, "I told you to get out of my class." Dreadfully embarrassed, I picked up my things and sheepishly slunk out of the room. The walk back across the green that September day did not seem as mild and sunny as it had a few minutes before. I was convinced that I would have the shortest college career on record, having attended less than one complete class. That was not the welcome I had imagined, nor do I recall the professor's name, but I can tell you that I never took another class from him.

After sulking in my dorm for an hour, I got up the gumption to go to my next class in the hope that I wouldn't get kicked out before it started. When I walked into Dr. Ochs's world history class, I got the impression that he was looking forward to meeting me because he greeted me with a big smile, a firm handshake, and a hearty welcome. Dr. Ochs had also gone out of his way to purchase a textbook for me before the bookstore ran out. He refused to take money for it as he "had an understanding with the bookstore." I felt instantly at home in his class. After class he got me caught up on what I needed to know and the readings I needed to complete. We talked about the time I had spent in the Soviet Union, which was the reason I was late for school, and that's when I found out that the Soviet Union was one of his specialties. Dr. Ochs left me with the assurance that I was welcome and that everything was going to be alright. During my two years there, I took a class from Dr. Ochs every semester. He offered interesting courses and was passionate about teaching, but his empathy first attracted me. Only later did I come to admire his knowledge, engaging style, and professionalism. Dr. Ochs caught me with the hook of the simple fact that he understood and cared for me.

After getting some help from the dean's office, I eventually was allowed into the English class. It was never a good situation because the teacher made it clear that he didn't want me there. While his hostility waned into indifference, he seemed to resent my very presence. I earned my "C" and was happy to never return to his class again.

Forgiveness

"Father, forgive them, for they know not what they do."

~ Jesus Christ

Empathy naturally leads to its corollary: forgiveness. Tapping into our natural inclination to empathize equips us to understand our students, laying the groundwork for forgiveness. Before we can forgive fully, we must understand fully.

The Christian tradition provides a powerful example of empathy and forgiveness. Jesus Christ experienced pain, suffering, and humiliation beyond description, having been betrayed, falsely accused, scourged, beaten, spat upon, demeaned, and a crown of thorns thrust upon His head. He was then subjected to the most excruciating form of execution known to the Roman Empire: crucifixion. The point of crucifixion is to kill the victim in the slowest, most agonizing means imaginable, with the motivation not being justice, but vengeance. Despite all that Jesus endured, some of the last words He spoke were, "Father, forgive them, for they know not what they do." To the end, empathy, mercy, and forgiveness remained the core of His character and an enduring legacy for His followers.

Did His executioners know what they were doing? In one sense, they did. You cannot strike a man, scourge him, place thorns on his head, or pound nails into his flesh by accident, so yes, they knew perfectly well what they were doing. In another sense, they did not fully know the impact of their actions. Jesus understood the ignorance of the offenders, and we can emulate that through empathy and forgiveness. In the case of those who crucified Jesus, what they did not know, what they could not know, where their innocence resides, is they did not understand the damage they were doing to themselves. Radical forgiveness believes that no one knowingly commits an offense when they truly understand what they are doing to the other person or to themselves. The child who screams at a sibling, "I hate you," has no idea what they are saying or why. When provided with empathy, forgiveness, and guidance, this child will come to understand and seek reconciliation because reconciliation is in our nature. In some cases, it was years before I realized the gravity of the wrongs I had done because I simply did not recognize them for the transgressions that they were. I meant no harm and yet I harmed, not out of malice, but ignorance.

Each student is at a different point along that path to adult maturity. Many students in their innocence have been misled by the media, a course culture devoid of civil discourse, and in some cases dysfunctional families, to believe that certain types of behavior are acceptable. They are told that short cuts, cheating, lying, vulgarity, and intimidation are acceptable behaviors as long as they get you what you want. Every day innocent students are bombarded with falsehood. They find it difficult to discern what real truth, beauty, and goodness look, act, and sound like. They are innocent victims of a world that bargains with the truth and accepts falsehood if the price is right.

This is where we must separate the action from the actor. Every student is capable of civil behavior, though some will have to unlearn destructive behavior. While we must forgive students, we do harm by ignoring or affirming behavior that is destructive to themselves and others. We must teach the truth, beauty, and goodness that flow from civil behavior. In short, we must be able to teach love, and a great place to start is through practicing empathy and forgiveness.

Abraham Maslow suggests, "We must understand love; we must be able to teach it, to create it, or else the world is lost to hostility and suspicion" (quoted in Montagu, 1975, p. 90). In so doing we begin to eradicate the debilitating effects of hostility, suspicion, and fear from our classrooms. Teaching love is best accomplished through our example: how we live before our students. Through forgiveness we model understanding the plight of others, while removing any ill will resulting from transgressions. We cannot change the past, but we can enlarge the future, through forgiveness.

Many teachers shared a piece of wisdom regarding forgiveness, summed up by Paul, a high school teacher, who remarked, "You never bring 'it' up again. When you're done you don't throw it at them ever again, it's over because every day is a new day."

Cheryl, a mid-school teacher, offers similar advice:

> I've had kids make some monumental mistakes in my class that they take responsibility for, and you know what, once it's done, it's done. I've never brought it back up again, not in a joking manner, not in any form ever, ever, ever, ever. When something of that magnitude and seriousness happens and it's been repented of and you've forgiven them, then it's done and it's never, ever, ever revisited in any form. That is true forgiveness, just letting it go. It would be demoralizing if I actually brought those things up to those students again in any form.

Not taking things personally can be difficult, but holding on to ill feelings, reliving unfortunate incidents, or holding grudges, only harms us as well as our students. These can permanently damage a relationship, making us all prisoners of a past that is best left behind. Forgiveness allows us to move forward unimpeded.

Scott, a high school teacher, shares his story about forgiveness and reconciliation.

> Last week a kid went off on me in study hall. He and another student were given the choice to be quiet or be separated. Through their actions they chose the latter. I finally said, "Okay, you move over there so you can stay away from him." He said, "Why me?" I said, "Because you're the one I chose." And he started to give me back talk and I said, "You've got about five seconds to be done with that. I don't want to have to send you to the office and you don't want to go. We don't want to make this into a big problem. Understand?" He definitely understood that I didn't need to say it five times. He grabbed me the next day and said, "I want to apologize." So I told him, "It's already out of my mind. It's done, you dealt with it and I really appreciate it and accept your apology." I have no problem with him whatsoever. We have too much to remember in the first place. You can't remember all that too.

We should have short memories when it comes to student misbehavior, understanding that students have bad days, make choices they regret, and say things they don't mean. Even with difficult students it is wise to empathize with their behavior and reset each day, believing that they want to do well, but they are still learning what it takes to make that happen.

Despite the seductive nature of revenge deceiving us into thinking that we can really drive home a point if we just exact a pound of flesh, the worst thing we can do when students misbehave is try to get even. If we are motivated by revenge, then students learn that revenge is acceptable adult behavior. Kelley recalls: "One of my college professors told me, 'If I could give you one piece of advice, it would be to never get revenge, because you are in a place that you have every opportunity to break someone down. Don't do it because you will always regret it.' I remember that. It's probably the best piece of advice I ever got." Forgiveness teaches our students an important lesson, is universally respected, and will impact students more than almost anything else we do.

In the world of digital communication some students feel more comfortable communicating through e-mail, text, or instant messaging. This is not an endorsement of communicating with students in this fashion, but a simple statement of fact. Chris, a high school teacher, talks about some advantages of these methods.

> I have found a lot of students are more comfortable texting or sending an e-mail to me. You know with e-mail kids will send me drafts of papers and other assignments. But I have also had situations where there has been a confrontation in the classroom and later the kid will send a message. I may have apologized, I may have said that I have understood and we need to move on from here. I remember one student who was border line cheating who sent me this guilt-ridden instant message. I responded back and said I understand—it's not that big a deal—I appreciate your apology—and let's move on. I think sometimes when they can put it in the written word without having that body language it sometimes can be very beneficial because you can express everything you need to say without being interrupted or reading their face and thinking they are not getting it. Sometimes that can be very, very valuable.

The message of forgiveness and reconciliation is important; the medium is optional. Openness to communicating with students on their terms helped Chris create a safe place where forgiveness and reconciliation were the norm.

Carla, a high school teacher, talks about the evolution of her classroom management plan and how, as her plan developed over the years, forgiveness seemed to become a natural part of it.

> As we talk about this I'm thinking, why would I not be forgiving? Why would I hold a grudge until the next day?

The thing is, if it's not dealt with fairly quickly then you might hold a grudge because it festers like a wound. To me it means having a well thought-out classroom management plan so there is a reasonable, natural consequence to any action. I feel like finally after so many years I've reached a place where I feel comfortable with what my plan is. As we follow the plan and the consequences are there, guess what—it's resolved. So forgiveness is built in.

I remember going home and thinking about certain kids and tomorrow I need to… But then you reach a point where you have a management plan in place that is perfected and forgiveness is easy because the issues have been dealt with. The consequences have been given and now we start over. I think a lot of times why you don't forgive is because you are holding grudges but it is more out of frustration because I don't know what to do with these kids. It's not that you don't like them and that you don't want to forgive, it's just that you are all upset and you are not sure what to do when all those things arise in class. There will always be conflict—now you have a way to deal with it.

Seeing students grow from past mistakes is gratifying. In the high school setting the adolescent who comes to us as a freshman is usually a very different young adult when they graduate. As students progress along their path to adult maturity it is important to recognize and affirm their growth. Pat, a school counselor, shares her perspective regarding forgiveness as it applies to students who make great strides during their high school years.

One very specific example often takes place during discussions for scholarships and National Honor Society applications. As a freshman a student may have done some boneheaded thing and you get in that meeting and discuss how this kid has grown from that experience. The kid admitted wrongdoing, took whatever the punishment was, and moved on. Many students have made National Honor Society or received a scholarship based on the fact that they came back from a mistake they made early in their high school career. I think that shows a very forgiving attitude on behalf of the faculty involved in making those decisions. Often the teacher that was involved may be the biggest advocate for that student.

What a wonderful way to communicate that through forgiveness we can enlarge the future.

Modeling contriteness and asking for forgiveness is also important. Jamie, a high school teacher, shares her thoughts on the importance of contrition.

I think admitting when I am wrong is important if I expect kids to do the same. Kids know I make mistakes and if I don't own up to my own mistakes that will really turn them off. They will begin questioning me as a genuine person who they can trust. So when I do something wrong I need to let them know that I am sorry, apologize, and say I was wrong.

Trust can be won or lost on the thinnest of margins. The trust of our students is one of the most important leverage points we have. Admitting mistakes and unabashedly asking for forgiveness is a great way to build trust.

In this next conversation, high school students talk about forgiveness, what it looks and sounds like, and the impact it has on them when teachers are forgiving.

"It's good to know you are forgiven like when a teacher actually says 'I forgive you.' Or when they ask us why we did something. Most often the teachers see what happened in a different way than students did. When they are willing to listen to what happened, talk about the infraction without a hint of retaliation, that feels really good."

"Most of my teachers understand good reasons for needing another chance. They understand my situation, or at least try. They try to understand why you are doing some of these things and they understand that you accept the consequences."

"They have to give consequences but hopefully without holding grudges. If it's the first time for something they move on, accept, and forgive. They allow you to learn from your mistakes and maybe even joke with you about screwing up. They forget the stupid thing I said yesterday and don't dwell on the past."

"It really helps me when they give you a second chance toward whatever you're working to achieve. Maybe even let me make the same mistake twice and letting you know that mistakes are not failures."

"It helps to realize that they make mistakes too. It's important for teachers to admit when they were wrong and you were right, when they apologize and say they are sorry."

"When you know you're forgiven it really lifts a burden off of your shoulders. It makes me feel relieved and grateful to know that no hard feelings are being held. I feel better about myself, it makes me feel respected."

"For me it makes me realize, hey, people can make mistakes and learn from them. It allows me to become closer with them, which allows me to learn."

"Knowing there are no grudges makes me want to try harder to rise above previous incidences. You want to do better and show them you're worth it."

"I respect them more and am more willing to forgive them when I am forgiven. I respect people with the ability to forgive."

Based on this conversation which describes many of the good fruits that flow from forgiveness, it is hard to imagine a downside. Extending forgiveness affirms our frail humanness. It teaches that mistakes are not permanent and that students can overcome errors, especially when they have the support of loving teachers. Forgiveness for students is the right thing to do because in most instances, they know not what they do.

WHAT STUDENTS AND TEACHERS SAY

"For all rapport, the root of caring stems from emotional attunement,
from the capacity for empathy."

~ Daniel Goleman

If I try to imagine what it is like being a kid growing up today, using my own childhood as the frame of reference, I am out of touch with reality. A summary of my childhood world would include family, sports, school, church, and the great outdoors. It was not a bad combination and I have no regrets. It is more difficult being a kid today due to the increased number of distractions and temptations. The bulk of the media our students are exposed to do not promote healthy human development, but rather glorify self-indulgence, foul language, unhealthy relationships, and violent and destructive behavior. Today's culture lies to our students about what constitutes truth, beauty, and goodness. We have a lot of work to do.

Because growing up is so challenging we must empathize with our students as they struggle along the path to adult maturity. I remember exhibiting my share of weirdness particularly through the middle of my teenage years. The following observations come from a conversation among middle and high school teachers as they talk about empathizing with students.

"I think it's important to understand them in terms of where they are developmentally. At the age of fifteen they are not going to act like they are twenty-five or thirty-five. But what does a fifteen-year-old act like? I think a lot of times we forget that. You work with these kids for many, many years and you still think they should be fully mature. But if you sit down and read in a psychology book, developmentally what does a fifteen-year-old really do? It's kind of like that mad cow syndrome, they are all over the place."

"The thing is that we have to remember that these kids are adolescents and they can act mature one minute and then one minute later they are kids again. That's part of growing up. I know it can be exasperating. I hear the complaints in the teachers' room, but I see so many different sides of these kids. I see the good and then fifteen minutes later I can see the bad. I just hope I never see the ugly. That sounds like a movie, doesn't it? But you have to realize they're still kids, this is their job and it's part of growing up. They exhibit multiple personalities because the peer pressure is so great. Yet they want to please us as long as their peers aren't around. But if they are with a certain peer, that has to come first because it's so important. So it just depends on who this kid is with how they are going to act. The pecking order is extremely important in high school."

"School is number one for us but not always for kids. This is not a judgment, it's just the truth. The fact is they have more going on in their life than being here. To us it is a profession, this is what our life is really all about right now, and for them they have a million other things on their plate so that school, a lot of times, is not in the top five of that million."

"One of the things that I'm learning I have to deal with more and more is understanding the baggage that they come with. This is a tough time of the year because a lot of my kids don't have much to go home to over Christmas. Like the homeless child who can't even fathom what it's going to be like because when they come to school they get a lot of support and two good meals a day. That may not happen again for a couple of weeks until we get back in school. So I try to give them a little more leash, try to be a little more understanding because there are so many other factors playing into their daily existence. I hope to always remember that. I'm trying."

"Students have more baggage sometimes than I think we do as adults. They bring so much with them and so many things that we wouldn't even know. Last year I know I had a couple of kids who, until partway through first quarter, I had no idea that they were homeless. When I think about it I guess my least concern would be, 'Can I pass my U.S. history test?' At that point in time my biggest concern would be, 'Where do I sleep tonight?' I think we have to be sensitive to the fact that they are human and many face issues we can hardly imagine."

You may have offered money to a student on a field trip who couldn't afford anything to eat or brought clothes to a student who was in need. You may have taken a student into your home for a time until they could get back on their feet. One of my heroes in life adopted a baby when one of her at-risk students gave birth to a child that she was unable to support. I'm not suggesting that these are requirements of the profession; I just know a lot of loving teachers who have done all these things and more. I know that you make accommodations for students when you become aware of a unique situation in a student's life. If a student is sick or has a family emergency the day before an assignment is due you don't say, "I'm sorry, there are no exceptions." You are far more likely to say, "Let's work on it—I'll give you another day." Even the Internal Revenue Service gives extensions without penalty. Modifying a deadline or an assignment is empathy in action. Empathy doesn't mean modifying expectations, but it recognizes there are many paths to the same destination.

We can show our empathy through the everyday practices, such as homework, that are part of the school experience. Let's assume we assign a short research and writing assignment that we expect students to hand in the next day. One student goes to a home with a small library, a computer with Internet access, and dinner that is served by one of her parents. There is a study space in her room and an assigned time to complete her homework in which her parents are available for advice. In all likelihood this student could complete almost any reasonable assignment. Another student has three younger siblings to take care of and is expected to cook the family dinner. There is no library, Internet access, study space, or time set aside to complete homework. While the parents may want to help their child, they may not have the time or ability to do so. This scenario plays out every day in our schools and homes. Can we reasonably expect the same results from these two students? Is there a structural inequity that we need to be aware of when we assign the same homework to students with very different resources and circumstances? We need to maintain high standards for all students while at the same time realizing that there are an infinite number of solutions to this dilemma. The solutions are grounded in awareness of the different challenges our

students and families face and the empathy to address these differences.

There are also times when homework should not be assigned. I learned from my high school math teacher, Jim Otte, to never assign homework during Homecoming week. While the purpose of Homecoming is not academic growth, it serves a social purpose that, outside of class time, is the focus for the week. Each school and grade level has times when homework will create more problems than it will solve. You may want to consider what those times are in your own situation. Homework is necessary as long as it is relevant and moves the ball forward for our students.

Kathy, a student, shared this interesting practice that her math teacher employs regarding homework.

> For math we have a forty-five-minute rule. If we have homework and it's really hard for us, we're supposed to spend forty-five minutes on it, and no matter how far we get we can stop and say that's all we got done. So we don't have to do it all. Our teacher doesn't want us to spend our whole night doing just the homework for his class. He knows we have other classes and other assignments we need to get done.

Obviously this practice is founded on trust, which in itself sends the message that we have faith in our students. It also reflects an awareness that students learn and work in different time frames and that each course a student is taking is equally important to a well-rounded education. Some schools alternate homework on specific nights to achieve the same end. The method is less important than the awareness and empathy involved in understanding that today's students lead extremely busy lives and that identical expectations in terms of the ability to complete homework assignments is inherently unrealistic.

Taking personally what students say and do is an obstacle to empathic behavior. Many times when students are disrespectful or grouchy it has nothing to do with us. We are bound to catch some stray voltage from various stressors in students' lives. Danielle, an art teacher, shared this story from a recent experience with one of her students.

> Don, who is usually a very laid back kid, had been a pill all week. On Thursday he needed to get some supplies from his locker and on his way out he made a very rude comment. I followed him out to meet him in the hall to give him the business but when he came back it occurred to me that maybe something else was eating at him. When he came back we sat down and I said, "Don, I've known you since you were in second grade and you have never treated me like that. What's going on?" Sheepishly he apologized and shared with me that his mom wouldn't let him go to the Homecoming dance and that made him really angry. We sat and talked about it and ended on good terms like we had always been. I was really going to let him have it with both barrels and for some reason thought better of it. I'm so glad I did; that could have permanently ruined our relationship.

Danielle's awareness that something was amiss with Don saved their relationship. By rising above her anger she was able to sense that there was more to the situation than a disrespectful, angry kid.

Shelley, a high school teacher, shares her insights about not taking student misbehavior personally.

> We are usually the last thing on the minds of our students. They are there to impress their peers, the girls, so what they do, I don't take it personally. Maybe sometimes I should but I just don't because it's like, this kid is doing this for some reason and God only knows why in some cases, but he or she doesn't mean anything by it. They are trying to impress somebody somewhere and I may not see it.

Linda talks about a gift that I wish we could all have: total attunement with the students we serve. She begins with awareness but I think there's more: a spiritual component that can only be observed and not explained. I have worked with many teachers like Linda. These people are born to teach; their ability to serve is imbedded in their DNA. "A teacher I worked with long ago used to meet a child and it seemed she was able to see right into their souls. She felt what they felt, knew their families and what was happening in each child's personal world and could communicate with them without words." We can all aspire to this level of awareness and empathy as we serve the students in our care. If you have this gift, trust it and use it.

Coach Andrist

"The weak can never forgive. Forgiveness is the attribute of the strong."

~ Mahatma Gandhi

Coach Andrist was highly competitive and expected the same level of commitment from his student-athletes. He understood that having a competitive attitude was an indispensable component in becoming a successful wrestler, but his competitive nature never interfered with his ability to empathize. When any one of us lost to a superior wrestler, despite giving our best effort, he was always supportive while coaching us how to do better next time. If we did not give our best effort, he still empathized in our loss but thankfully refused to sympathize because that would have meant abandoning his expectations for excellence.

As a sophomore I entered the finals of the conference wrestling tournament undefeated. I had easily beaten my opponent earlier in the year and took this match too lightly. The result was a humiliating 5-0 loss. Coach knew I had not prepared myself properly and that I had not given my best effort; thus, he had no sympathy for me. Because of my lack of focus and preparation I got what I deserved and Coach was very explicit in pointing that out. At the same time Coach understood that no fifteen-year-old performs at their best every day. While he pointed out my lack of preparedness and effort, he did not dwell on it. We concentrated on preparation for the following week when I would likely meet this same wrestler in the regional finals. The focus for the week was not on recent failure, but preparation for future success. Coach forgave me for my poor effort and I was able to move on with a well-earned lesson in humility. I was able to reverse my fortunes and win the regional tournament because we did not focus on past mistakes, but through Coach's help, we enlarged the future.

AVOID HOSTILITY

"A loving heart is sensitive to the whole of life, to all persons;
a loving heart doesn't harden itself to any person or thing."

~ Anthony de Mello

When students try our patience there is a temptation to reply with hostility, put them in their place, or, worst of all, get even. If you have experienced these impulses but not acted on them, you obviously are equipped with high degrees of self-awareness, empathy, and forgiveness. The following stories describe a degree of hostility that no student should ever experience. In each case the witnesses describe enduring consequences, some good and some bad. In the first story Mike, a master teacher, shares an experience from his middle school years that continues to negatively impact his life.

> Let me tell you a story from my eighth grade year. I'm a horrible singer; I have a horrible voice and I couldn't carry a tune in a bushel basket. We had to sing for our Christmas program and I would always mouth the words because I am so tone deaf that you could clearly hear me when we would play the tape. It was really embarrassing to listen to that tape so I knew enough to just mouth the words. I learned to cope. We had a new eighth grade teacher that year. She made me stand up in front of the class and I had to sing an entire song from the Christmas program. Then she had everybody vote, "Do you want Mike to sing or do you not want Mike to sing?" They voted and of course nobody wanted me to sing. That happened to me in eighth grade and to this day I can't even sing in church. That experience is still so powerful in my mind that when it comes to singing I have this awful visceral reaction.

Even when I go to church every Sunday I just cannot sing. I can't work up the nerve to do that.

A number of things strike me about Mike's experience. A lot of students "learn to cope" like Mike did. They may not be doing exactly what we want them to, but they adapt and do the best they can with what they have. Adapting is a high-level skill. Mike's adaptation was not unreasonable. The heartbreaking aspect of this story was the teacher's humiliating response. We can think of a dozen different ways she could have handled the situation and still involved Mike in the concert. Sadly, she chose a method that was heartless and hostile.

Chad shares another mid-school experience involving choir class (no pattern intended).

When I was in middle school choir, it was a required class, and it wasn't really my cup of tea. Because I didn't really want to be there I exhibited behaviors accordingly. I just remember the consequence for exhibiting those inappropriate behaviors was so severe and strong. I remember a handful of my hair dropping off the teacher's hand because that was the consequence—grab the hair and shake it and being told to behave until the hair came out. This happened in a small town where I couldn't really avoid her. I lost all respect for her as a person. I probably did deserve some kind of consequence, but I felt that was a little bit overboard.

I also was a paper boy and this lady was on my route. Like I said you just knew everybody and that really turned me off to who she was. I actually dreaded going to her house to collect money from her for the paper. I would see her on the street and it wasn't that I was afraid of her; I just felt so much animosity and really a sense of hatred toward her. But there it was, in a small school we would run into each other and she would look the other way. I had no intention of being a teacher at that point, but I know that is one of those things that I am cognizant of, not so much the physical abuse of a student but just what is it that is going to make so-and-so hate me. I'm not so worried about them liking me, but I definitely don't want a student to hate me.

I had two teachers in middle school who did the same type of thing. One twisted your hair until you kneeled down and begged. The other had a big class ring that he turned over in his hand and bopped you on the head. Students do not learn from teachers they don't like (Aspy and Roebuck, 1977).

Cheryl's story and insights emphasize the connection between self-awareness, empathy, and forgiveness as well as alluding to the importance of being a real model.

> Sometimes I am really disappointed in listening to conversations in the teachers' lounge. Last week I listened to a colleague telling a story about a kid who happened to be studying for a math test during his English class. Obviously that was first and foremost on the child's mind. The teacher said, "I told the child to put the book away, and I turned around and the book was still there, and so I walked over and picked it up and threw it across the room." And I thought, okay, how many times have I seen you grade papers during faculty meetings? That kid at that moment was very concerned about an upcoming math test and you just communicated very clearly several things about anger and lack of control. Every now and then teachers are masters of sarcasm and can be brutal with their sarcasm. Sometimes it is playful bantering back and forth, but I have also witnessed teachers cut kids to ribbons and I have known kids to break down crying.

Of the many responses available to this teacher, throwing the student's book across the room falls in the "not top ten."

A WORD OF ENCOURAGEMENT

"Wisdom is to be sensitive to this situation, to this person, uninfluenced by any carryover from the past, without residue from the past experience."

~ Anthony de Mello

Self-awareness, empathy, and forgiveness involve significant intellectual effort and courage, but the benefits for us and our students are incalculable. Getting into our students' "quality world" (Glasser, 1990) involves both awareness and imagination. We must continually reflect on the accuracy of our understanding and the paradigms through which we view our students.

Acting in ways that support our students often takes courage. Forgiveness makes us vulnerable to criticism for being soft or enabling our students. I encourage you to empathize and be forgiving anyway. It takes a special person to truly see and understand from another person's perspective, and an even bigger person to realize the innocence of people who truly cannot see the truth about their behavior. Through empathy, forgiveness, and re-direction we help students understand the negative consequences of their behavior, thereby enlarging their future. There is a space between being a doormat for others and being an unreasonable tyrant. In that space is the wisdom and courage required to empathize, understand, and forgive.

"Could a greater miracle take place than for us to look through each other's eyes for an instant?"

~ Henry David Thoreau

Chapter Nine: Respect

WHY RESPECT IS LOVE AND WHY RESPECT MATTERS

"Respect is love in plain clothes."

~ Frankie Byrne

The root word for respect, *respicere,* means to look at or to see. Through the eyes of love, we see our students as they are, respecting the unique nature of each student, accepting them unconditionally despite their imperfections. Our students are not objects whose existence is meant to fulfill our needs. Quite the contrary: they are unique creations whose individuality we are committed to nurturing. Respect requires that we see every student anew each day and discern and meet each student's needs. The push back we sometimes experience from our students is not primarily a refusal to comply with school standards; it is the yearning of the human spirit for the freedom to actualize its potential. Respect involves educating in a fashion that does not inhibit, but rather emboldens the blossoming of each student in their unique nature, and along their unique path.

For most students, particularly adolescents, respect is synonymous with love. Students yearn to have their thoughts, opinions, creativeness, and ability to solve their own problems acknowledged and supported. Learning opportunities that allow students to display their unique abilities is one aspect of respect. Respect is also communicated through a considerate tone of voice, receptiveness to student communication, confidence in student abilities, trusting that students are giving their best effort, honoring their humanity, bolstering their esteem, and genuine listening. Treating students with respect enhances academic achievement and is a disposition that is highly valued by students (Larivee, 2000; Deiro, 1996).

When we offer knowledge but not respect, our knowledge is often rejected, not for the lack of its utility but because the messenger is perceived as flawed. We can only presume a student's respect when we are respectful, because respect is earned through our actions, not conferred by our position.

Respecting each student's unique talents, dreams, ambitions, and aversions requires courage in the face of the standardization taking place in the American educational system. There is great danger in attempting to make each student identical in behavior, aptitude, perspective, and accomplishment. This defies nature while diminishing the singular talents and perspectives that each student possesses. Nor does standardization reveal the unique contributions each student is equipped to provide to society as a whole. The industrial school model reinforces this notion of uniformity to the detriment of our students and the society at large. Uniformity of input and output may serve adults well, particularly political types who have done more damage than good to the American educational system. Sadly, our current model subverts the flowering of individual achievement and ambition: hallmarks of a free nation. Respect for the individual is a cornerstone of a broad based classical education and the American way of life. Promotion of mindless uniformity only results in the greatest of human tragedies, unrealized human potential.

"Teenage Punk"

"What we see in the love relationship is a fusion of great ability to love and at the same time great respect for the other and great respect for oneself."

~ Abraham Maslow

Tammy, a high school senior, shares this story.

My junior year, kids met with a college counselor and she made suggestions on what we would want on our résumé and stuff. We were like thinking out loud about community service ideas that we could do and my student teacher offered something that would be a great service project. She knew we were capable of doing it and that we could do a really good job with it even though it would take a lot of commitment. She was working with the lost boys from Sudan and she trusted us and encouraged us to help her with the project. It was a lot of work but we all learned so much through that experience. We got to speak with these boys who wandered through the desert for two years. We helped them get housing and jobs and raised money to bring other boys to the United States. She helped us in so many ways and knew what we were capable of doing. She was a true believer. If she would have thought of us as teenage punks I doubt she would have taken us on in her work. She treated us as adults.

Students thrive when we take the leap of faith to provide them with meaningful opportunities to serve. Tammy was a young lady who faced serious personal challenges of her own, but despite these issues, her student teacher respected her abilities and commitment by offering a meaningful and challenging service-learning project. Tammy grew a great deal through the experience and respected her teacher for providing the opportunity.

LOCKER ROOM CONVERSATION

"He who confers benefits will be amply enriched, and he who refreshes others will himself be refreshed."

~ Proverbs 11:25

Sometimes the smallest comment we make carries the most weight with our students. Randall shares a story about his basketball coach who voiced his respect for Randall's strength as a team leader. The teacher may never have known the mutual respect this simple comment engendered in Randall.

> After a morning practice Coach was just standing in the hall socializing with other students when he stopped me and said, "I really thought what you had to say in the locker room this morning was really important and I really value your opinion. You showed great leadership. Thank you for contributing." At that time anything nice out of his mouth was really cool because our team didn't hear a lot of it. And so it was something that was really special to me.

When asked how his coach's respect affected him, Randall responded, "Ever since then I really appreciated him as a teacher and I valued his classes a lot. I valued his opinions a lot more and I just listen to him a lot more because he respects me. So I guess I feel like if I have his respect then he definitely has mine." Randall became more engaged in class, not because the teacher had changed any aspect of his teaching, but because he treated Randall with respect.

RESPECT AS BELIEF AND FAITH

"Men are respectable only as they respect"

~ Ralph Waldo Emerson

Faith in students can start at a very young age, as we learn from Amy, a high school student, who shared this story.

When I was in first grade, Ms. Hoekstra, my kindergarten teacher, sought me out and asked me to come back to the kindergarten to speak about a certain topic. I was really into dinosaurs and I just happened to know a lot more than the average kindergartner or first grader. So Ms. Hoekstra asked me to come to her kindergarten class and share with her students what I knew about dinosaurs. When I was a first grader and was asked to teach younger students about something, that was one of the coolest things I could think of. Just being respected like that and to go to the younger classes and talk was a really great experience for me. Because of that I've never had a problem speaking in front of groups. I guess when you start young that makes a difference.

Ms. Hoekstra respected Amy's knowledge, even as a first grade student, and thereby provided an opportunity for Amy that produced positive results and established an enduring relationship of mutual respect.

RESPECT AS FORGIVENESS

"Forgiveness does not change the past, but it does enlarge the future."

~ Paul Boese

Respect includes the understanding that we all make mistakes that require forgiveness. Forgiveness does not mean endorsing everything our students do. Like us, students are on a perilous journey called life that is fraught with difficult decisions and sometimes we just get it wrong. When students make mistakes, even big mistakes, rather than responding with anger or resentment, perhaps the right response is merely disappointment. We need to differentiate right from wrong but we also need to isolate condemnation of the act from the actor.

Jill, a student, shares the following story of forgiveness and respect.

> I have taken quite a few vocational courses and am taking another one this semester. I am also a teacher's aide down in that department for Mrs. Smith. A few weeks ago we printed a few shirts up at the school print shop that were very suggestive. I guess that's the word that best describes the shirts. After we got in trouble for wearing the t-shirts, me and two other kids had a meeting with the principal and Mrs. Smith. And even after we basically smacked Mrs. Smith in the face to make this shirt, I mean we did everything secretively, she still said all this good stuff about me to the principal. I was just kind of amazed that she still had all this respect for me after what we did. We had to make up for it, but she never held a grudge for what we did.

Mrs. Smith was able to subordinate her ego and separate the actor from the action, while supporting her students in a time of need. The forgiveness and respect offered by Mrs. Smith surely enlarged the future for Jill.

"LOSE MY EGO."

"To be humble to superiors is duty, to equals courtesy, to inferiors nobleness."

~ Benjamin Franklin

During pep assemblies and athletic events, student behavior can get a little edgy because these events promote boisterous behavior. On the one hand we encourage our students to cheer loudly for their classmates, while at the same time expecting our students to do so in a respectful fashion. There is certainly a wide range of opinion about what constitutes respectful and appropriate behavior at sporting events, one man's cheer is another man's jeer. Sadly, our culture seems to tend toward jeering. Student inventiveness is often one step ahead of the rules we apply in these circumstances. When we tell students they cannot do X they come up with Y, which is often some slight modification of X but still just enough of Y to not have violated the rule about X. I do not envy those in charge of crowd control at today's sporting events.

Paul describes a situation which really challenged him:

> Sometimes I just have to lose my ego. If I am wrong, I just need to seek out those who were involved and apologize. An example was when I was enforcing a rule from the administration about student behavior at a basketball game. We were playing our cross-town rival. The students were all dressed up and really wired for the game. The gym was just electric. When I reprimanded a group of students some of them contradicted me in a less than appropriate manner. I went to check with the assistant principal and found he had indeed rescinded the rule they were breaking without telling us. Well, I went back and apologized to this group of students in the presence of the liaison officer who wanted them to apologize or he was going to ticket them for their behavior. He was surprised that I would do that, even though it wasn't really my fault. He eventually understood the reasoning and the rest of the evening went off without further incident.

By checking his ego Paul did not needlessly jeopardize his relationship with these students. Paul concluded by saying, "I had several of those students in class and almost every one told me how much they appreciated my apology. What could have been a real deal breaker turned out to be a relationship builder with some of those students." We tend to get what we give. By showing respect for these students Paul opened the door to a mutually respectful relationship.

What Teachers Say

"All serious writers on the subject of ideal or healthy love have stressed the affirmation of the other's individuality, the eagerness for growth of the other, the essential respect for his individuality and unique character."

~ Abraham Maslow

Respect for the individuality of students includes respect for their thoughts and opinions. One of the most disrespectful actions we can take is to "blow off" a student who is willing to offer their insight. Our dismissiveness leads students to shut down because they wonder "what's the use if they won't listen anyway?" As one student shared with me, we should be willing to listen "no matter how ignorant we sound when we are saying it." The key word here is ignorance, not stupidity. There is always more that we don't know than we do know. All of us are largely ignorant about a good many, if not most, subjects. A more effective response to a bizarre comment by a student is to question respectfully, in order to help the student clarify their own thinking. This is how meaningful learning takes place: one human mind to another. I am not suggesting that we should agree with all student opinions, but respectful dialogue is a key to learning and a wonderful way to model civil discourse which is woefully lacking in our culture. The following segment derives from a conversation between master teachers on the topic of respect.

☙

"I believe communicating love is all about building relationships with and showing students that they, as well as their ideas, are respected. They are intelligent, intuitive, and enlightening individuals who have taught me many lessons over the years. Respect is a two-way street, and students are perceptive, they know the difference between respect and patronizing behavior. Respect means being there for them without judgment, no matter what, to challenge, praise, encourage, and listen."

"I had the privilege to work with the most wonderful colleague for over twenty years. She was so well respected because I never heard her say a cross word to a student. She treated every student with the utmost of respect, and of course, they responded to her. It was a very, very unique relationship that she had. Kids knew that she cared about them without being their buddy. They knew that she wanted them to do well and she helped them in every way that she could, but she wouldn't give them a free ride. But just her interactions, she always had a smile, she always had something positive for kids. I think teaching with her and being around her in the last few years I have started to model more and more of her behavior, and it has paid off big time for me in my relationships with my students and in how they achieve."

"I think a good classroom community is based totally on respect. If you can have that sense of community, have an egalitarian approach where every student is an equal and that every student's opinion is valued, where there is no artificial hierarchy, and then respecting their input and making it a comfortable environment for everyone. When that happens, and it is no easy task to accomplish, then good things start to happen for everyone. We just had that election. There were a lot of very controversial issues and believe me my students were not shy about voicing their opinions. It was a great opportunity to model valuing the comments that might not be the ones everyone wants to hear."

"Respect, that's my number one lesson with the daily reflection I have them keep in a binder. I ask them to make an entry in the journal section of their binders. I'll ask them a question, have them write on it for a few minutes and then ask, 'Well, what have you got?' Kids that I never hear anything from content-wise are almost always the first to speak up when it comes to an opinion about moral issues like slavery or civil rights questions. Not only do they see when injustice occurs, they want to make sure you understand what they think is right. It really opens them up. This provides a great opportunity to validate them, the position they take, and the reasoning they provide. And even if their reasoning isn't always real clear I think they appreciate the chance to be heard. It just seems like those issues of justice and injustice, they are all over it. Respecting their opinions and thought processes is very important to them."

"One other big thing is when you are wrong and you don't admit it. You might try to push it off or even try to make it their fault. You need to say, 'That was mine. I made a mistake here, and let's get it right.' Or 'I'm sorry I did that. I apologize.' It could even be in humor. Sometimes you'll say something that you think is really kind of funny but you realize later that maybe that sarcastic remark that was supposed to be funny was really hurtful to this student. Instead of just blowing it off thinking they'll be fine I need to pull them aside afterwards and say, 'I'm sorry about that. I didn't mean for it to come off that way.' But I think not respecting students, even inadvertently, is something we need to be aware of and how it can affect students. I think it really breaks down communication tremendously between the students and the teacher which is never a good thing."

"We had a presentation Friday by some Hmong students about their culture. They did it so well that they had the entire class eating out of their hands. They brought a ton of cultural artifacts that none of the other students had seen before. Everybody was just riveted with what they had to share and they had so many questions that a ten-minute presentation took the entire period. It just felt good to sit back and watch it happen and I was very moved myself. They just took over and you could feel the learning happening and a lot of understanding and respect for one another. That was very good."

"In Student Council too I think we show respect for students when we put them in charge of an activity whether it be Homecoming, Snow Fest, or anything else that we plan. There is a clear message of respect when we can share the responsibility and put them in charge of big projects. It's not just taking part in the activity but organizing it for the entire student body. The word 'ownership' is a reflection of respect."

This conversation reinforces my belief in the American teacher. These teachers demonstrate the awareness, insight, compassion, and respect that is the foundation of our professional ethic.

WHAT STUDENTS SAY

"Love is the ability and willingness to allow those that you care for
to be what they choose for themselves
without any insistence that they satisfy you."

~ Wayne Dyer

The following is a conversation among students discussing the topic of respect.

☆

"We realize that teachers have to be in charge of the classroom. That's part of their job. But it's always nice when we get to make some decisions, even small ones. This week Mr. Brown asked us, 'Do you want to take the quiz on Friday or should we go for Monday? Before you answer that question you are going to need to provide some reasons for putting it off.' We had a great discussion about the pros and cons and he eventually put the quiz off until Monday."

"With our Student Council advisor she gives us a lot of chances to make decisions. And not just about Prom and Homecoming. She will ask about, even in the school level, things like, 'What do you see? What could we be doing different here to make this a better place for students?' It's neat because she is actively seeking our opinion and asking us about everything happening in school. We are so used to us asking the teachers questions about what might be right and wrong. But she is always asking us what we think about the environment here and how could we change this? I think that shows a lot of respect."

"I've had that happen in the classroom level too. Sometimes Mr. Pearce gives us questionnaires about how things are going in his class. He'll ask questions like, 'Should I try to do this experiment next year or was it a waste of time?' Or, 'Do the reviews help you for tests and how do I need to change them if they don't?'"

"And also if you are going in before or after class, they realize that you actually want to learn about what they are teaching. It makes them happier because they want you to like what they are teaching. So they get to talk about it and then you get to learn about it. They respect you more because they know that you want to learn about that subject."

"I agree. It's kind of like a respect that you would have for your parents. Like if your parents ask you to do something and they say, 'You need to have it done by this time.' Well, if you don't have it done, if you are a human being at all, you would feel some remorse. You would feel kind of upset that you did it to your parents, that they wanted it done and you didn't do it just because you didn't feel like it. It's kind of like a family in school, a big family."

"I like it when they give you respect for your efforts. If you do homework the best you can, like on tests for math if you do most of the work but you still get wrong answers, you still get points for doing a lot of the work. Respect for at least trying hard is important to me."

"When they respect your choices. Like you've made the choice that you aren't going to participate in something, they'll give you the respect of making your own decisions. They respect that you're old enough to make your own choices. Or they respect your choice to take on more responsibility in class through a special project that you might be real interested in but is a little off the beaten path. And sometimes that works out real well for a quiet student who hasn't been doing much and all of a sudden they say, 'You mean you're going to let me do that?' When that happens other kids see them in a different light, too. It lets them shine."

⟐

Students and teachers cite nearly the identical teacher actions as respectful behavior, including giving students a voice in their own education, validating students' reasoning skills and perspectives, assisting students beyond regular class time, promoting a learning community or family type atmosphere in the classroom, apologizing, and listening. All of these communicate respect in the eyes of both students and teachers.

Coach Andrist

"A youth is to be regarded with respect. How do you know that his future will not be equal to our present?"

~ Confucius

One of the most difficult experiences for a coach is to have a student-athlete quit the team. The sense of loss is profound and difficult to not personalize. There are always those nagging doubts for a coach: what did I do wrong, how could I not see this coming, did I do something that pushed this athlete away from the program? On the other hand, there is also the temptation to blame the athlete. He wasn't tough enough, he lacked dedication and discipline, or, we didn't need him on the team anyway, I'm glad he quit. In most circumstances none of these speculations are true. Most student-athletes don't quit because of the coach or some personal character flaw, they quit because they no longer enjoy the sport, have found other interests, or have grown in a way that the sport no longer holds the same appeal.

When I was a junior, one of our seniors, Dick, a good friend of mine and a guy who was having a very good season, quit the team in the middle of the year. Without saying a word, he just quit coming to practice. Dick had wrestled all through high school, would have been competing for a conference championship, and was an important part of our conference championship team. Dick quitting was inexplicable to me. When he quit, Dick began avoiding everyone on the team including Coach Andrist.

To his credit, Coach never took Dick's actions personally. Within a few days he sought Dick out to talk to him. He did not disparage Dick's decision nor try to persuade him to come back. Coach's sole purpose was to reassure Dick that he still respected him and that, whether he wrestled or not, it was not going to impact their relationship. He respected Dick, not because he was a part of the team, but simply for who he was. Coach thanked him for the contributions he had made over the years and wished him well in whatever he chose to do. Coach Andrist knew that wrestling was not for everyone and that at some point we all move on to other things.

For Dick it came at a very unique time, halfway through his senior year. It takes a big man to respect a decision like that and not take it personally. Coach Andrist respected Dick enough to make sure that Dick's choice did not negatively impact their relationship.

Avoid Arrogance

"The truest characters of ignorance are vanity,
and pride and arrogance."

~ Samuel Butler

Arrogance is one of the biggest turn-offs for students because it presumes a superiority which is the antithesis of respect. The following conversations (with intermittent commentary) come first from teachers, and then students. The topic is arrogance. Craig, a high school English teacher, shares the following experience from his high school years.

> I was a freshman, a country kid who went to a big school. It happened in algebra class and I still remember the guy's name. On any given day he would be in your face almost like the drill instructor at boot camp. He would say to me and other students, "You've got the brain of a gnat!" It harmed my self-esteem and really discouraged my studies in his class so much that I had the opportunity to do it again the next year. So, I failed algebra. I hated math! He stayed with the district for a long time. My younger brother, six years younger than me, has wondered in conversation how many people's lives that guy screwed up. Teachers like that give the rest of us a bad rap and they mess with countless students.

Craig mentally dropped out, or more accurately, was pushed out, by the arrogance of his teacher. How invested would any of us be if we were told that we had the mind of a gnat? Thankfully Craig had a resilient personality and moved on to become a master teacher.

I had a very similar experience because I had a math teacher that would say disrespectful things to me my junior year. "Oh, you scored more points in your game last night than you did on your quiz!" Well, I had 3 points the night before. So he said that in front of the whole class. We'd be called to the board to do problems and I would stand there and it took me so long to do them. He would be up there saying "tic-toc, tic-toc, we don't have much time." I remember getting done with that class and just thinking, "I'm an idiot." So I didn't take advanced math my senior year. I got to college and I had to take calculus but I thought I was so bad in math that I would never make it. But then the calc teacher just loved what he was doing and I'd go in for extra help and he was very encouraging and all of a sudden math became possible for me. I actually liked it. But in high school I shut down in math for a whole year. I had no respect for the math teacher or for myself.

Arrogance causes some teachers to be dismissive of students' abilities. This teacher's arrogance had the effect of making his students feel small.

"Mine was a math teacher too. My second semester in college I had a calculus class and on the very first day the teacher was up at the board explaining something when a student raised her hand and asked a question. The teacher just flew off the handle. 'That is the stupidest question that you could ever ask. I can't believe you would ask that. Where did you go to school?' She just ripped the kid apart. So we went through the entire rest of the semester without a single student asking one more question. I'm pretty sure that's what the professor was looking for, no more questions. That lack of respect just shut the entire class down."

"We had a teacher who basically took advantage of the relationship with the students to get tickets to the Final Four in Minneapolis. This student had access to the tickets and got them for this teacher.

Then the teacher turned around and sold the tickets at a profit. He scalped them. He weaseled his way for some tickets taking advantage of his relationship with a student. It wasn't the only time that he did that, where he took advantage of relationships with students. And although I think a lot of times kids liked him, I don't think they ever respected him. It was horribly unethical for a teacher to do that. It was just a rotten thing to do for a person to prey upon that perceived friendship. And of course word got out what happened. Any respect that he had vanished."

◡

A scam like this demonstrates arrogance and lack of respect for the sanctity of the student-teacher relationship. This is an example of seeing a student as an object to further a personal agenda instead of a pupil to be served.

The following is a conversation where students share their insights regarding teacher arrogance.

◡

"I think a lot of times that they will ignore some of your questions or maybe just try to ignore anything that you say. Then of course it makes you want to just give up in the class and makes you not care about the class."

"If you are having problems with something, they will sometimes say, 'Well, we already learned that,' instead of trying to go over it again with you. They say, 'You should already know this kind of stuff.' Maybe we did cover it in class, but that does not mean I learned it. You are kind of confused and don't know what to do and they're not helping you. It seems like the only students who get respect from teachers are the ones who get it the first time."

"I think some teachers have that sort of air about them, that they're the ultimate in school here and that we need to be idolizing them and giving every ounce of respect to them. I think it should be more on an eye-to-eye basis instead of us looking up to them constantly. They should be able to relate to us. I think I heard one time something about earning respect."

"It's not really the information that they are giving; it's more that they are selling their personality, I think. The units and the activities can be really exciting but it's more like how they present the material like personality wise. If a teacher doesn't respect you, if they are arrogant, even if the class is interesting at times it's a major turn off for me."

☩

Teachers and students both affirm that arrogance is a turn off to learning. When we diminish others, we sabotage our own efforts as educators. Yes, we have to be leaders who need a level of confidence to perform well, but we should do so humbly, realizing that there is always more that we don't know than we do know, and respecting that our students take many paths to the promised land of actualizing their potential.

A WORD OF ENCOURAGEMENT

"Only those who respect the personality of others can be of real use to them."

~ Albert Schweitzer

As our students travel the path of self-discovery, finding their places in this world, they will inevitably make some unproductive detours as we all have. The good news is that these detours are often fertile ground for discovering what does and does not work. Part of our job is to respect these choices and, to the degree we can, help students learn from them.

Some students don't need to touch the stove to know that it's hot. For others only the pain of touching the stove will do. Some students are adventurous; others are more cautious and have a natural aversion to risk. Some are outspoken, others are more reserved. The permutations on this theme are infinite. Be bold in respecting the unique nature in each student because that nature is there for a reason that we may never understand. The tapestry of the human experience is made more beautiful by the variety and uniqueness of each individual.

"Respect is not fear and awe; it…[is] the ability to see a person as he is, to be aware of his unique individuality. Respect, thus, implies the absence of exploitation. I want the loved person to grow and unfold for his own sake, and in his own ways, and not for the purpose of serving me."

~ Erich Fromm

Chapter Ten:
The Big Finish

FOUNDATION

"When it is approached as a dynamic process, we can understand
the acute need for love, not only by the infant and the child but by
adolescents and adults, since denial of love, as we are now discovering,
may block the attainment of our human potentialities, stunt our
personalities, and prevent our maturation."

~ Lawrence K. Frank

The evidence is overwhelming that "Love makes us who we are, and who we can become" (Lewis, Amini, and Lannon, 2000, p. viii). Understanding and applying this simple but profound fact of human nature is the key to fulfilling our mission to promote the full healthy development of our students. Love is the answer to the question that asks, what is the foundation on which we build our professional practice? Should the foundation be the latest academic standards, technology integration, skills for the 21st century, Project Based Learning, the Common Core State Standards, or maybe Expedition Learning? There are many trendy choices out there; take your pick. All are negotiable afterthoughts that in the absence of a loving school culture will have no more influence on promoting human development than any other gimmick. No matter what approach we choose, if the foundation does not begin and end with the universal human need to give and receive love, then the rest doesn't matter.

We must love what we do, who we do it with, and who we do it for. When these are in place, everything is possible. When they are absent, even the smallest obstacles will frustrate our efforts.

WARNING: LOVING IS THE MOST CHALLENGING THING WE DO AS EDUCATORS

"This attitude—that nothing is easier than to love—has continued to be the prevalent idea about love in spite of the overwhelming evidence to the contrary."

~ Erich Fromm

Loving requires overcoming our egos and our inclination for self-serving behavior that is part of our survival instinct. There is a persistent and seductive call that we all hear which tries to convince us that we are the center of the universe and that everything was created to serve our existence. Overcoming this aspect of our nature is challenging, and because it is so challenging, it provides a great reward.

In our efforts to love our students we are going to experience "failure," in the form of committing unloving acts. Most will be small; a look of disgust or a word spoken in frustration; and a few may be horrific. Failure has been defined as the opportunity to start over more intelligently. For our purposes we will define failure as the opportunity to start over more lovingly.

The following story illustrates a fall that to some degree, albeit not this severe, we have all taken during our career. It is not the fall that is the real story, because we are all going to fall, it is how we respond to the fall that matters.

"Shit For Brains."

"My will is to love everyone. I really want to love everyone. However, my actual state is that I do not love everyone. So now I want to learn how to love more people."

~ Anthony de Mello

A physical education class is finishing its workout for the day in a cramped, dank weight room in the school basement. The primary apparatus is a Universal weight machine, but there are also assorted free weights scattered around the room wherever they can find a resting place. The tired students were asked to finish up and hit the showers. One young man has one more movement in mind. He starts to "skin the cat" on the pull-up bar. The teacher notices that his feet are going to hit the one light bulb in the room which is positioned above the bar. He tries to alert the student to the impending accident by saying, "Don't do that! Stop, stop, stop!"

POP! Just as the teacher suspected, the student's foot shatters the light bulb, scattering shards of glass across the weight room floor. The teacher snaps and screams at the student, "Didn't you hear me? What do you have, shit for brains?"

Silence. A totally dejected student stares blankly at the teacher with the eyes of a wounded doe. He had meant no harm. The other students, after a passing look of pity at the young man, look at the young teacher with bewilderment. The stunned students slink out of the weight room, silently trudging off to the showers. The dejected young man tries to speak but cannot find words to match the painful situation. Crestfallen, he follows the other students to the locker room in silence.

The young teacher stands alone, ashamed, paralyzed, unable to comprehend his inexcusable reaction to such a trivial matter. He begins to slowly sweep up the pieces of broken glass knowing that more than a light bulb has been broken. He has belittled a fine young man and subjected his innocent classmates to a spectacle of dehumanization that no one deserves. The incident is tragic for everyone involved. Everyone is a loser.

The young teacher drives home, muddles through dinner and a night of staring at, but not really watching, television. He wonders, "What do I do to make this right?" He commits to apologizing sincerely and unconditionally for his misbehavior. He will ask for the forgiveness of every student in the class, and more specifically from the chastened young man. He knows that he may not be forgiven. But he knows he must do his part to set things right.

The next day the young teacher sincerely, unequivocally, making no excuses, apologizes to the class as a whole and each student individually. That was a start. Re-earning the trust and respect of the students would take more time. The young teacher learned a valuable lesson and thankfully never repeated that behavior again.

We all fall at one time or another, saying and doing things of which we are not proud. Only one course of action can have any meaning in these times when we shame ourselves by shaming others, and that is to sincerely and unconditionally apologize for our actions, seeking but not necessarily expecting forgiveness. Kids understand and are forgiving, particularly when we model forgiveness, or in this case, humility and contrition. There is nothing wrong with admitting that we have fallen short of the standards that we expect of our students. It would be a huge mistake not to admit it, and delusional to think we will never fall.

Shocking as it may sound, the majority of our students have not experienced a lot of truly loving relationships in their lives. Erich Fromm (1956) suggests, "No objective observer of Western life can doubt that love…is a relatively rare phenomenon, and that its place is taken by a number of forms of pseudo-love which are in reality so many forms of the disintegration of love" (p. 77). Most have experienced pseudo-love through dependency, co-dependency, or manipulation. Young men and women are very used to the subtle message of "I will love you if…" This is not love; it is manipulation or worse. If what Erich Fromm suggests is true, when students experience true love, it may be foreign to their experience and they may respond with skepticism. Be patient, persevere, and do so with the full knowledge that you are operating from the highest nature of your being and that love never fails.

THE ROAD LESS TRAVELED

"Two roads diverged in a wood, and I—I took the one less traveled by, and that has made all the difference."

~ Robert Frost

Because we are created for love, being a totally loving person is something we all aspire to become, either intentionally or unintentionally. So we wonder, "How do we get there?" or perhaps more accurately, "How do we become love?" Pitirim Sorokin, in his classic work *The Ways and Power of Love* (1954), suggests that most loving altruists follow one of three paths to that Promised Land.

The "early-fortunate" altruists are those who seem to be born with creative altruism. Just as some are born with musical or athletic talent, the "early fortunate" seem to have deep love for others as part of their natural make-up, being blessed with the grace to love effortlessly. The second type is the "late-converted" or "catastrophic" altruists. For these there is typically a seminal event in their lives that causes them to re-evaluate their ego, values, and associations. Often they make a drastic change in one or all three of these areas of their lives, intentionally choosing to pursue a more loving path. The third group is probably the most common. Sorokin describes these as the "intermediate" type. The natural tendency toward altruism is not strongly evident for at least part of their life. There are often events that change their outlook and behavior, these do not tend to be seminal moments, but rather the change is gradual, perhaps even evolutionary over time. For them, creative altruism does not come as naturally as for the "early-fortunate" nor is there a single snapping of the twig through which enlightenment occurs as it does for the "late-converted." I encourage you to examine your own life in considering which path may be yours. The road we take matters not; the importance is the destination.

There is comfort in considering Sorokin's three paths to altruism for ourselves and our students. Very few are going to be "early-fortunate" altruists, but each of us can develop our capacity to love through courage and will. Each of us, including our toughest students, can develop the awareness, will, and ability to love unconditionally, and so realize the highest state of our being. The path will be alternately easy and difficult, but the reward is a guaranteed happy conclusion which begins by choosing the path less traveled.

In summarizing the impact of altruistic love, Sorokin writes, "Viewed from this standpoint, unselfish love is not only a life-giving force, but is also the best therapeutic method for securing real peace of mind, meaningful happiness, real freedom and creative power. The almost unfathomable possibilities of unselfish love remain practically untapped by contemporary science" (Sorokin, 1954, p. 200). Love is a life-giving force leading to the highest reaches of human experience promoting peace of mind and happiness. Love does not coerce, but rather, promotes freedom and the uniqueness of the individual. Love is goodness combined with fearless strength; therefore, the more we love, the stronger we become. "Hence, the scientific prescription. The most effective and most accessible way to acquire the maximum of constructive power is to love truly and wisely" (Sorokin, 1954, p. 12).

As we apply this wisdom to our professional walk it becomes stunningly clear that the love we bring to our classrooms is the single most important influence in promoting the full, healthy development of our students. Our nature beckons us to follow this road less traveled because the evidence suggests it will make all the difference.

BLESSINGS

"The main aim of education should be to produce competent, caring, loving and lovable people"

~ Nel Noddings

The stories from previous chapters reveal many blessings that naturally flow from a loving student-teacher relationship. Because love is the universal catalyst of healthy human development we identify the development of these potentialities as blessings, the good things derived from loving and being loved. There are no liabilities derived from love, only assets of the most exquisite kind. We identify the three main blessings resulting from Teacherly Love as goodness, well-being, and development.

Teacherly Love has the tendency to promote goodness and loving behavior in students, without diminishing the source from which the love originated. There is an abundance mechanism about love, guaranteeing that the more we love the more love and goodness grows in those whose lives we touch. Loving teachers act as models to help students grow in love for self and others.

Being an object of unconditional love contributes to one's physical, social, emotional, and spiritual well-being. Being loved makes us feel good about ourselves, our circumstances and the world in which we live. For students it has the added effect of making them feel good about their school, teachers, classes, and the pursuit of knowledge. A mind at peace is an inquisitive mind open to all possibilities. A mind free from fear is the pinnacle of well-being.

We speak of development in the broadest terms, to include what is often described as the whole child: mind, heart, body, and spirit. This is our calling as professional educators, as professionals in the human development business: to help young men and women realize their full potential in every aspect of their lives. Love does not place limits on human development, but rather, gives free rein to each individual to pursue their dreams in a manner conducive to their unique gifts.

Goodness

"The evidence suggests that the status of a loving human being is the most important and desirable that a human being can achieve. To produce loving human beings should be the primary purpose of education, all else should be secondary to that purpose."

~ Ashley Montagu

All of us at one time or another have said, "He is such a good kid," in part because we value goodness as highly as we value any other attribute in our students. In "goodness" we value the ability to love well and wisely. Goodness denotes empathy, compassion, integrity, honesty, high moral character, and a willingness to sacrifice one's own interest for a greater good. When we say, "She's a good kid," we are referring to some form of loving behavior. When students experience Teacherly Love, they make comments like the following:

"It makes me want to continue working because I feel I have a purpose in life and makes me want to learn more so I can teach others."

"It makes you feel special and makes you want to carry the kindness on to others."

"I don't want to let down a teacher who believes in me so I work extra hard to succeed for myself, which is also a victory for them."

"It makes me have a lot more respect toward them and honor them more as a person and to try and see where they're coming from."

"You come to respect them and to want to be a good person."

There can be no doubt that when we are real models of love, we help our students grow in goodness. For my own children I value goodness above every other attribute because it means they have developed an enhanced capacity to love. When they discover what they love to do, they will throw their whole being into developing the skills necessary to be successful. Because they know how to share love, they will never be without it in their lives. What they share with the world will return to them. Love is the state of being that requires nothing else to make one whole. Love is ultimately a gift from God. As the ultimate herd animal, goodness is what makes us most human, providing us with everything we need for a fulfilling life. Supreme Court Justice Clarence Thomas once said, "Good manners will open doors that the best education cannot." Goodness, even more than intellect, is an attribute that brings peace of mind, helps us develop mutually satisfying relationships, and attracts opportunity, taking us to what we most desire.

Creating the Culture

"We don't know how to love except by learning from being loved."

~ Lawrence K. Frank

We have a great opportunity to model goodness to our students through how we live before them. Peter describes the reciprocal and environmental impact of modeling goodness in his classroom.

> When I think about how it affects students when teachers love their students, they reciprocate that. When you ask "How's it going," and treating them with respect all of a sudden they say, "May I please go to the bathroom?" Those kinds of things seem to naturally happen. When you're saying, "Could you please move that table over there? Great—thanks—I appreciate that." Alright then they will say, "May I please get a piece of paper from you?" I'm not saying everybody needs to say please and thank you all the time, but it becomes a part of the culture in the classroom. I guess you could call it a culture of love or respect. The whole environment changes and kids naturally act better. Deep down every student wants to be good, do the right things.

Perhaps our greatest influence comes from modeling simple courtesy which is a most important and enduring character trait. It is also a blessing for us; when we develop a culture of goodness in our classrooms, everything else becomes possible.

Well-Being

"In practically all my subjects where data were available, this tended to point to the conclusion that (all other things being equal) psychological health comes from being loved rather than from being deprived of love."

~ Abraham Maslow

Love promotes well-being and is the antidote to fear and anxiety. Children who are at peace with themselves and are comfortable in their own skin are equipped to learn and love. While fear and anxiety inhibit development in all facets of life, being free of anxiety enhances our ability to think clearly and problem solve. Feelings of hope, optimism, peace, and joy enhance intellectual development. Laughing and joking enhance critical thinking and problem-solving skills, making the mind predisposed to alternatives from a positive perspective. The opposite holds true. Anxious students tend to become more cautious and disposed to giving into fear. These outlooks of helplessness and despair impede intellectual development. The neural circuitry of the brain dictates that emotional states impact our ability to think rationally and clearly. When students experience high levels of anxiety or other negative emotions, they can have difficulty focusing or processing information clearly and accurately (Goleman, 1995).

Students expressed their well-being to me in the following ways:

> "It makes you feel positive about the subject and the teacher and really good about class. Like there's a reason I am here in school."

> "It makes me feel like I belong here and that I am part of something."

> "It boosts my confidence academically and personally. I feel better about myself, so then I want to achieve more."

> "I end up in a good mood when I am done in their class. It makes me feel good to be in a happy environment."

> "I feel good about myself. I feel like I can do anything!"

> "It makes you believe in yourself and gives you more confidence in yourself."

For my own children I want them to grow in goodness and well-being because I know that development in all other areas will naturally occur when their goodness and well-being have developed. Give me a student who has a healthy sense of self, a positive attitude about learning, is a good-hearted person striving to do the right things, and I guarantee they will do well in whatever area they pursue.

"WHY WOULD YOU CARE?"

"The entire world seems hypnotized in the wrong direction—encouraging us to love things rather than people, to embrace everything new without noticing what's lost or wrong, to choose fear instead of peace. We promise ourselves everything except each other. We've forgotten the source of true contentment and well-being."

~ Margaret Wheatley

Sadly, some students we serve have what might be called a "love deficit." They have few, if any, genuine experiences of love in their lives, so when they encounter love, it can be foreign to them. Cindy teaches in a small, isolated community in the Rocky Mountains. Her story illustrates how a simple act of love can promote the well-being of our students.

"Shane came to us from a big town in the Midwest. He had spent most of his school years moving from one town to another, living with different members of his family. It seemed to me he felt like a 'throw away child' and it was easy to understand why. He was a very nice young man but was extremely anxious about school, being hesitant to try new things or even turn in work he had done. With the way the world had treated him, his low level of trust was understandable. He just did not feel comfortable with his situation or identity.

"Because he had bounced around so much I don't think he ever really had a good experience in school. He was very bright but it was obvious there were significant deficits in his learning. At his previous school he was a C student. When I asked him about his experience there he told me the main issue he faced was not getting beaten up every day. The expectations in his classes were quite low. He didn't really have to do anything. As long as he didn't cause any problems he was pretty much guaranteed at least a C for a grade. Well, in our little school the academic expectations were quite different and it took him some time to adjust.

"Shane had been gone for a couple of days and when he came back to class I asked him, just as I ask every student, how he was doing and if he was feeling 100% or was he still not quite up to par? His answer stunned me. He said, 'Why would you care?' He wasn't being facetious or disrespectful, he was genuinely surprised that anyone would ask him about being gone from school. My impression was that no one had asked him that before and that he was genuinely interested why I would ask. I went on to tell him why I cared about him, the positive attributes I saw in him, and why he was important to me. It took some time and a lot of effort on both our parts but eventually Shane developed into quite a good student. The biggest change for Shane was that he eventually developed some self-worth. After that everything else fell into place. He took his studies more seriously, was willing to take risks and embraced challenges rather than hiding from them. I think because he knew we cared for him he began to care for himself."

The Sanctuary

"The positive and negative sets of facts well confirm that the grace of love is indispensable in forming the sound, integrated, and creative personality. This constructive function of love is one of its many forms of power."

~ Pitirim Sorokin

Many of us have very positive elementary school experiences that remain almost idyllic in our memory. Cassie, a high school math teacher, describes such an experience and how it informs her professional practice today.

I remember one of my favorite teachers was my fourth grade teacher. Every day after lunch it was a section of our day when it was time just for us. She had taken a special spot in her room and made it warm. She threw a carpet down and we all got to just relax and be. She'd read to us every day for like half an hour and she was just so very warm. She had us relax, lay back and picture in our minds the scenes from the books she read. I just remember really enjoying that time and it was comfortable, relaxed and it just felt like a very safe environment. It was like being home in front of the fire. She had made it very safe and therefore it was very pleasurable.

When I think about that and after thinking about how students realize we love them, it occurred to me it is not my words so much as my actions, the environment, and the time we spend together. I want the time that my students spend with me to have at least some of that same experience. I always set aside some time to focus on my students and their well-being and on other non-academic related issues. Because they are high school math students I don't read to them in the corner but sometimes we just share things or ideas that are important to us without any judgment or criticism. We relax and are just happy to be with each other.

Some might be critical of the "off-task" behavior Cassie describes, but when we understand how important the feeling of well-being is to our students, this is time well spent. Exploring the big ideas with our students—their dreams, their place in the world, their questions about life—provide context for learning. Exploring ideas free of judgment and criticism is the ideal environment for learning and promoting a healthy sense of self. Human development is not about creating automatons that all think and act alike. It is about discovering our gifts and turning those gifts into masterpieces.

Development

"People tend to achieve their human potential insofar as they develop love and reason."

~ Erich Fromm

In our examination of development, we are referring to the whole child, to every aspect of a student's life, not just academic performance. While we tend to measure the efficacy of the American educational system only through student performance on high stakes tests, here we will cast a wider net in an effort to more accurately reflect the nature of the human condition.

We have a natural tendency toward wholeness, self-actualization, and positive growth, all of which are promoted through loving relationships. As Carl Rogers suggests, "Briefly, as a person is accepted and prized, they tend to develop a more caring attitude toward themselves. A higher sense of self results in greater levels of actualization and positive growth. Man's natural tendency is toward positive growth. Only in an unnatural state, characterized by negative regard for self, does destructive growth occur" (Rogers, 1980, p. 116).

Maslow (1964) suggests that American education is conflicted about its goals and purposes. We have become value-neutral, characterized as purely technical training or the acquirement of pure knowledge for its own sake. Both approaches limit the actualizing tendencies of students since each does little to provide meaning in the larger context of the human experience. A comprehensive education should develop all human capacities, not just the cognitive ones. Maslow writes, "The far goal of education—as of psychotherapy, of family life, of work or society, of life itself—is to aid the person to grow to fullest humanness, to the greatest fulfillment and actualization of his highest potentials, to his greatest possible stature" (p. 49).

A value-free education that does not fully address human nature is incapable of producing these results. The ultimate goals of the American education system must include "spiritual values" or "higher values" that address truly important questions such as "What is the good life? What is the good man? The good woman? What is best for my children? What is justice? Truth? Virtue?" (Maslow, 1964, p. 52). Through addressing the whole child, we have the "possibility of winding up with a usable normative concept, i.e. that education is 'good' which best 'beautifies' the student; i.e., helps him to become more honest, good, beautiful, integrated, etc." (Maslow, 1971, p. 134). Maslow proposed that the highest goals for American education, just as they are for fully actualized people, should include Being-Values (B-Values), including truth, goodness, beauty, wholeness, dichotomy-transcendence, aliveness, uniqueness, necessity, completion, justice, order, simplicity, richness, effortlessness, playfulness, and self-sufficiency (p. 129). The value and meaning of an education goes well beyond the reading, math, and occasional science scores that currently drive the educational machine.

The following statements from students reflect how a loving environment promotes development in all aspects of their lives.

"It makes me more cheerful and positive toward learning and about life."

"It makes me feel like I can achieve things for that teacher; I want to make them proud."

"It makes me want to try much harder, to prove to them that I really have it in me."

"It allows you to grow more as a human being because if one person believes in you, you should believe in yourself."

"I treat my teacher as a valued member of the school community."

"You want to work harder for your future."

"It allows for learning beyond curriculum."

You may look at Maslow's Being-Values and ask, "How do we measure those?" I don't have an answer for you. Perhaps someone else does. However, when we address these values, values that are more important than a student's ACT or SAT score, the natural result will be an explosion in academic performance. As students actualize their full potential as human beings, their goodness, search for truth, aliveness, playfulness, order, simplicity, self-sufficiency, and so on, their academic progress will naturally occur. The problem with standardized tests is they only measure test-taking ability and what we might call "student-ness." They have little, if any, predictive value for "do-itness," or "human-ness." In addressing the needs of the whole child through love we are nurturing at the root of human development, not hacking at the branches represented by the test, standards, or philosophy *du jour*.

LOVE CHANGES EVERYTHING

"It (love) is a force that can be the most powerful agent in the classroom, leave the most lasting impression, and touch lives most deeply"

~ Nel Noddings

In describing the impact of love, Chris, a high school science teacher, really gets down to the basics.

> They are in my class. I deal with students who have a history of disaffections with school but they seldom miss my class. They feel they have ownership in class and belong. Therefore they find success at some level in school. The "rough" kids will listen if they know they have a voice. They are making better choices and realize they are responsible for their choices. For me it is my actions and commitment of time beyond the contract or what is expected. I focus on the students, not other adults.

"They are in my class." There is no doubt that if we can keep students in our classes they will learn, achieve, and grow. Recall that a roughly 30% drop-out rate in American schools is one of our "root" challenges. We are naturally attracted to love. Students who feel loved will not walk out our doors because love is what keeps them coming back, not the text books, not the reading or math program, and certainly not the testing program. They come back because of the love, the aliveness that you and I share with them. From my own experience I can tell you that I performed for the teachers who loved what they did, who they did it with, and who they did it for. There were days when I didn't feel like practicing, but I wasn't going to let Coach Andrist down so I went and gave my best. I absolutely didn't like English class, but I sure liked Mrs. Werth so I went and tried to get interested. Mr. Baltz was so crazy I didn't want to miss any of his antics, and it would not have mattered what course he was teaching. Dr. Ochs bought me a book for crying out loud, how could I miss his class? Math…schmath…I went to math class because Mr. Otte was one of the funniest people on earth, not because I was captivated by polynomial equations. The human element is and has always been the key element in education. Only you and I can provide the love that students crave; we are the decisive element in the classroom. *Who* we offer as a loving person is more important than *what* we offer.

I would like to revisit how Kari, an elementary teacher, elegantly describes the impact of love on the development of her students.

> Love changes everything. Stephen Covey says, "Begin with the end in mind." The "end" I envision for my students is one in which they have become good-hearted people with strong character, avid readers, competent problem solvers, and enthusiastic lifelong learners. I know, however, that those things don't just happen in an individual's life. I must enthusiastically teach and model those skills and behaviors I hope to see in my students. But without a platform of love, good instruction has no place to land. The Apostle Paul said, "If I speak in the tongues of men and of angels, but have not love, I am only a resounding gong or a clanging cymbal." If I do not first, and consistently throughout, demonstrate and express love, my students cannot receive even the most eloquent instruction. Teacherly love truly changes everything! Feeling and being truly loved impacts students' involvement, engagement, level of belonging in the group, how they and their parents view school, how

they view themselves as a learner, and ultimately whether or not they experience success. The impact, therefore, of being loved by your teacher cannot be underestimated.

Kari's description is so insightful, comprehensive, and self-evident, it defies further analysis, making this a good place to end.

"Nothing resists the truth for long: it may be assailed, but never overcome."

~ St. Ignatius Loyola

Personal Epilogue:
The Long and Winding Road

"It (love) bears all things, believes all things, hopes all things, endures all things."

~ Paul the Apostle

In the personal prologue, I described my relationship with Coach Andrist and the gifts he shared with me. In my senior year and the following summer, these attributes brought about a meaningful and satisfying experience in my life. My personal mission and the focus of our professional relationship had been to win a state wrestling championship.

In my senior year, my record was 30-0 and I was wrestling in the semi-finals of the state tournament. This was my third state tournament and I was the number one rated wrestler in the state at 155 pounds. The dream we had worked so hard to achieve was two matches—twelve minutes—away. But dreams don't always come true. In this case, it turned into a nightmare of sorts. For the first time in my life, I was pinned in the first period of the semi-final match. Losing the semi-finals of the state tournament was bad enough; being pinned for the first time ever was awful. I spent the rest of that day in a surrealistic fog. I could not, or would not, recover from the disappointment of that defeat. Looking back, I see that I lacked the resiliency of character to bounce back from that defeat and compete to the best of my ability. I lost my next two matches and finished a disappointing sixth in the state tournament: a far cry from the goal we had worked so hard to achieve.

As an adult looking back on that experience, it is easier to see the relative insignificance of losing a few matches. In the larger scheme of things, I was still alive and healthy, had a family that loved me, and was in charge of the rest of my life. It was not like I was a refugee in a war-torn land. But for a seventeen-year-old kid, this was, up to that time, the most disappointing day of my life. I felt like I had let down my friends, my family, and my beloved coach. I was convinced that I had squandered all the years of their support in one afternoon. While they were all comforting and supportive, I was not mature enough to acknowledge or appreciate their efforts. I crawled inside my misery and wallowed in self-pity. My immediate reaction, and for some time thereafter, was that I was done with wrestling, that I wasn't good enough to wrestle at the college level, and that I could not bear the thought of going through that kind of disappointment again. I decided to cut my losses and move on to other pursuits. As far as wrestling was concerned, I quit.

Through it all, the belief, faith, and support of my family and Coach Andrist never wavered. While he was as disappointed with the outcome as I was, he was not disappointed in me. He continued to love and support me, and believe and have faith in me despite what I viewed as a lack of evidence that would support such a conclusion. Coach Andrist's career was never based on individual or team success advancing his personal agenda or coaching career; he used wrestling as a vehicle to develop young men into mature young adults.

Wrestling season turned into baseball season and the disappointment of that day faded as all disappointments do. Nevertheless, I was unwilling to consider pursuing a college wrestling career. Even thinking about wrestling was painful and I continued to believe that I did not have the right stuff to compete at that level.

Returning to the three gifts that Coach Andrist shared with me: they were vision, high expectations, and being a real model to emulate. Although I had let him down, he continued to share these gifts with me. Coach knew me well, understanding that being an athlete and specifically a wrestler was part of my identity, even when I denied this part of my being. While never employing an "in your face" approach, Coach persistently talked to me about college wrestling as part of my future. The intermediate vision of being a state champion was gone, but he still endorsed the longer range ambition of wrestling at the college level, an ambition that I had dismissed. His high expectations for me never diminished. He also modeled the maturity, optimism, and realism that I lacked. I viewed the state wrestling tournament as a defining event punctuated by failure. Coach viewed the state tournament as a single disappointing event, an experience along the path rather than the destination.

Baseball season was over, graduation came and went, and I had yet to secure a summer job; (the truth was that I hadn't looked all that hard). Coach talked me into wrestling in a local freestyle tournament, which led to the state freestyle tournament, which led to a five state regional tournament, which led to the National Junior Olympic Tournament in Omaha, Nebraska. Didn't Bilbo Baggins say something about the danger of stepping out your door, you never know where you'll be swept off to?

Sometime in late June there was also the National Age Group Freestyle Championships in Cedar Falls, Iowa. While successfully maintaining self-imposed unemployment, there was no good reason to not make the drive south and give that a go. Competing better than I had in my entire career, wrestling top athletes and state champions from all over the country, I only lost one match that summer. While Coach was not able to attend most of these competitions, he was always there in spirit. His years of guidance equipped me to mentally and physically prepare for each match just as if he were by my side. His gift of love provided me enduring blessings beyond time and space.

It was late July and I had won the National Age Group Championship (18 years of age and under) in Iowa and had finished as the runner-up at the Junior Olympic National Championships (19 years of age and under) in Omaha. It was an unexpected dream summer of wrestling, but things had the prospect of getting even better. I hadn't known that the winners of each of these national tournaments were going to compete for the opportunity to represent the United States on the first ever junior national cultural exchange team to the Soviet Union. It all came down to a two-out-of-three match series to determine if I would earn the honor of representing my country on a cultural exchange team competing in the Soviet Union.

Isn't life funny? Within months of what was the most disappointing day of my life as an athlete, I was once again within two matches—twelve minutes—of realizing a goal that Coach and I had worked toward for so many years. We had dreamed of a high school state championship, but now, out of the blue, something even better had come our way. Often great opportunity follows on the heels of great disappointment, and yet there was a hollowness about it. I was hundreds of miles from home with no friends or family to share the joy of the experience.

This was unquestionably the *Be There* (Chapter Three) moment in my life. My father and Coach Andrist drove all night from Weyauwega, Wisconsin, to Omaha, Nebraska, to *be there* for me when I needed them most. I had been in a similar circumstance a few months earlier and fallen flat on my face. Believe me, I saw the parallel in the circumstances at the time. Despite a summer of successful competition, old doubts and fears beckoned. I was close once before—was I going to choke again? Was I going to let my father, my family, and my coach down again? Would this be *deja vu* or redemption? Thankfully, one of the beauties of love is that it drives out all fear.

I can't adequately describe the assurance I felt when the two men I admired most, and whose faith sustained me, showed up unexpectedly that morning. Their presence helped me make the leap of faith from hoping I would win to knowing I would win. While love had endured all things through disappointment, it also believed all things on this day. It didn't matter who my opponent was, it could have been a tag team match against the Banack brothers with Dan Gable thrown in as a kicker, I was going to win those two matches and for no other reason than the love, belief, and faith my coach and my father had in me. My faith had wavered but theirs never did.

The result was the experience of a lifetime. I was honored to represent my country as a member of the Junior National Wrestling Team on a month-long cultural exchange in the Soviet Union just five months after I had given up on myself and wrestling. Thank God my coach and my family never did.

The three gifts Coach Andrist shared with me during those formative years have sustained me through challenging times for my entire life. Because he knew and understood me well, he was able to remind me of my identity and kept me connected to my mission. Because he was persistent and never gave up on me, I continued wrestling that summer and for the next five years in college. His vision and high expectations for me, while not realized as a high school state champion, were realized as a Junior National Champion. In my years as a teacher, coach, principal, and superintendent, I have tried to emulate, sometimes successfully and sometimes not, the values and ideals that Coach Andrist teaches and lives by. When I coached, I endeavored to do all those things that Coach Andrist had done for me. As a superintendent, I still see myself as a coach whose prime responsibility is human development, growing the capacity of those in our organization to more effectively serve the needs of our students and their families. In short, I hope I am growing in my own capacity to love.

Coach Andrist became my champion by first capturing my heart. Once that was accomplished he got the rest of me—mind, body, and spirit. Some of his actions could and should be considered heroic, well beyond the normal expectations of a teacher or coach. But most of what he did were small things, small things done with great love. Coach Andrist helped create the very best aspects of who I am today. For that I am eternally grateful.

My encouragement to you is to be a champion for the students in your care. Love your students in a fashion that reflects your own uniqueness and beauty. Don't try to imitate another person's style; you've got your own style. Connect with each student personally, professionally, and through "who you have to offer." Your "who" is beautiful, loving, compassionate; your excellent qualities are embedded in your nature. You were born to love and be loved. Let your better nature be your guide. Love each student and the rest of the details will take care of themselves.

> *"Love seeks one thing only: the good of the one loved.*
> *It leaves all the other secondary effects to take care of*
> *themselves. Love, therefore, is its own reward."*
>
> ~ Thomas Merton

Bibliography

Ackerman, Thomas, ed. (1997). *Educating Throw Away Children: What We Can Do to Help Children at Risk.* San Francisco: Jossey and Bass.

Armstrong, T. (1994). *Multiple Intelligences in the Classroom.* Alexandria, VA: Association for Supervision and Curriculum Development.

Aspy, D. N., & Roebuck, F. N. (1977). *Kids Don't Learn From People They Don't Like.* Amherst, MA: Human Resource Development Press.

Banard, B. (1995). *Turning the corner from risk to resiliency.* Portland, OR: Western Regional Center for Drug Free Schools.

Beishuizen, J. J., Hof, E., van Putten, C. M., Bouwmeester, S., Asscher, J. J. (June 2001). *Students' and teachers' cognitions about good teachers.* The British Journal of Educational Psychology: Leicester.

Blanchard, K., & Johnson, S. (1982). *The one-minute manager.* New York, NY: William Morrow.

Bonner, D., & Aspy, D. (1984). A Study of the Relationship Between Student Empathy and GPA. *Journal of Psychology,* 149-153.

Brophy, J. E. (1981, May). On praising effectively. *Elementary School Journal, 81,* 269-78.

Burnett, P. (1999). The Impact of Teachers' Praise on Students' Self-Talk and Self-Concepts. ERIC Document No. ED431768.

Buscaglia, L. (1982). *Living, Loving & Learning.* New York: Random House, Inc.

Buscaglia, L. (1984). *Loving Each Other: The challenge of human relationships.* New York, NY: Holt, Rinehart and Winston.

Cole, A. D. (2003). It's the teacher, not the program. *Education Week 22*(26), 33.

Cothran, D. J., & Ennis, C. D. (2000). Building bridges to student engagement: Communicating respect and care for students in urban high schools. *Journal of Research and Development in Education 33,* 106-17.

Covey, S. R. (1989). *The 7 Habits of Highly Effective People.* New York: Simon & Schuster, Inc.

Covey, S. R. (2004). *The 8th Habit.* New York, NY: Fireside: Simon & Schuster, Inc.

Crump, C. A. (1996). Teacher Immediacy: What Students Consider to be Effective Teacher Behaviors. Research Report. ERIC Document No. ED390099.

Davis, G., & Rimm, S. (1989). *Education of the Gifted and Talented.* Upper Saddle River, NJ: Prentice-Hall, Inc.

De Mello, Anthony, (1990). *Awareness: The Way to Love.* New York, NY: Random House.

Deiro, J. A. (1996). *Teaching With Heart: Making healthy connections with students.* Thousand Oaks, CA: Corwin Press.

Dickmann, M. H., & Stanford-Blair, N. (2002). *Connecting Leadership to the Brain.* Thousand Oaks, CA: Corwin Press, Inc.

Dweck, C. (1999). Caution–Praise Can Be Dangerous. *American Educator 23,* 4-9.

Escalante, J. (1990). The Jaime Escalante Math Program. *Journal of Negro Education, 59*(30), 9.

Fay, J., & Funk, D. (1995). *Teaching with Love & Logic: Taking control of the classroom.* Golden, CO: The Love and Logic Press, Inc.

Feshbach, N. D., & Rose A. (1990). Empathy and aggression revisited: The effects of classroom context. Paper presented at the biennial meeting of the International Society for Research on Aggression. Banff, Alberta, Canada.

Flanders, N. A. (1961, December). Analyzing teacher behavior. *Educational Leadership 19,* 173-80.

Fromm, E. (1956). *The Art of Loving.* New York, NY: Harper & Rowe.

Gardner H. (1993). *Multiple Intelligences.* New York, NY: Basic Books.

Garmston, R. (2000). Glad You Asked. *Journal of Staff Development 21*(1), 73-75.

Ginott, H. (1972). *Teacher and Child: A book for parents and teachers.* New York, NY: The MacMillan Company.

Glasser, W. (1990). *Quality School: Managing students without coercion.* New York: Harper & Row Publishers.

Glasser, W. (1993). *The Quality School Teacher: A companion volume to the Quality School.* New York, NY: Harper Perennial.

Goldenson, R. M. (1970). Psychology, psychiatry, and mental health. In *The Encyclopedia of Human Behavior.* (Vol. 1). Garden City, NY: Doubleday & Company, Inc.

Goldstein, L. S. (1997). *Teaching with Love: A feminist approach to early childhood education*. New York, NY: Peter Lang.

Goleman, D. (1995). *Emotional Intelligence: Why it can matter more than IQ*. New York, N.Y.: Bantam Books.

Goleman, D. (1998). *Working with Emotional Intelligence*. New York, NY: Bantam Books.

Good, T. L, & Brophy, J. E. (1972). Behavioral expression of teacher attitudes. *Journal of Educational Psychology, 63*(6), 617-24.

Good, T. L, & Brophy, J. E. (1971, August). The self-fulfilling prophecy. *Today's Education,* 52-53.

Greenough, W. T., Black, J. E., & Wallace, C. S. (1987). Experience and brain development. *Child Development, 58*(3), 539-555.

Hoyle, J. R. (2002). *Leadership and the Force of Love: Six keys to motivating with love*. Thousand Oaks, CA: Corwin Press, Inc.

Johnson S. (1998). Hug Therapy. *Children and Families 16*(2), 8-9, 11.

Keating, K. (1983). *The Hug Therapy Book*. Minneapolis: Comp Care Publications.

Kierkegaard, S. (1962). *Works of Love: Some Christian reflections in the form of discourses*. New York, NY: Harper and Row.

Kohn, A. (1991). Caring Kids: The Role of Schools. *Phi Delta Kappan,* 7-27, 496-506.

Larrivee, B. (2000). Creating Caring Learning Communities. *Contemporary Education 71*(2), 18.

Lewis, T., Amini, F., & Lannon, R. (2000). *A General Theory of Love*. New York, NY: Vintage Books.

Madden, L. E. (1997, Winter). A call for strength: How to manage students for a more caring society. *Education, 118*(2), 225-228. Retrieved December 3, 2003, from Montana Library Network – Academic Libraries.

Maerhoff, G. I. (1996). *Breaking Ranks: Changing an American institution*. Reston, WA: National Association of Secondary School Principals.

Marzano, R. J. (1992). *A Different Kind of Classroom: Teaching with dimensions of learning*. Danvers, MA: ASCD Publications.

Maslow, A. H. (1962). *Toward a Psychology of Being*. Princeton, NJ: D. Van Nostrand Co.

Maslow, A. H. (1964). *Religion, Values and Peak Experiences*. New York, NY: Viking Press.

Maslow, A. H. (1971). *The Farther Reaches of Human Nature*. New York, NY: The Viking Press.

May, R. (1953). *Man's Search for Himself*. New York, NY: W.W. Norton & Company.

May, R. (1969). *Love and Will*. New York, NY: W.W. Norton & Company.

McCaslin, M., & Good, T. (1996). *Listening in Classrooms*. New York, NY: Harper Collins.

Mendler, A. N. (2001). *Connecting with Students*. Alexandria, VA: Association for Supervision and Curriculum Development.

Montagu, A. (1953). *The Meaning of Love*. New York, NY: Julian Press.

Montagu, A. (1975). *The Practice of Love*. Englewood Cliffs, NJ: Prentice-Hall, Inc.

Noddings, N. (1992). *The Challenge to Care in Schools: An alternative approach to education*. New York, NY: Teachers College Press.

Palmer, P. (1983). *To Know as We Are Known*. San Francisco, CA: Harper and Row.

Palmer, P. (1998). *The Courage to Teach*. San Francisco, CA: Jossey Bass.

Peale, N. V. (1967). *Enthusiasm Makes the Difference*. Pawling, NY: Foundation for Christian Living.

Peck, M. S. (1978). *The Road Less Traveled: A new psychology of love, traditional values and spiritual growth*. New York, NY: Phoenix Press.

Perkins, H. V. (1965, January). Classroom Behavior and Underachievement. *American Educational Research Journal 2*(1), 1-12.

Pritchard, A. (2009). *Ways of Learning: Learning Theories and Learning Styles in the Classroom*. New York, NY: Routledge.

Ratey, J. (2008). *Spark: The revolutionary new science of exercise and the brain*. New York, NY: Little, Brown and Company.

Rogers, C. R. (1980). *A Way of Being*. Boston, MA: Houghton Mifflin Co.

Rogers, C. R. (1983). *Freedom to Learn for the 80's*. Columbus, OH: Charles E. Merrill Publishing.

Rosenthal, R., & Jacobson, L. (1968). *Pygmalion in the Classroom: Teacher Expectation and Pupils' Intellectual Development*. Norwalk, CT: Crown House Publishing Company, LLC.

Rowe, M. B. (1986). Slowing Down May be a Way of Speeding Up. *Journal of Teacher Education 37*(1), 43-50.

Rubin, T. I. (1983). *One to One: Understanding personal relationships*. New York, NY: Viking Press.

Rubin, T. I. (1990). *Real Love: What it is and how to find it*. New York, NY: The Continuum Publishing Co.

Rubin, Z. (1973). *Liking and Loving: An invitation to social psychology*. New York, NY: Holt, Rinehart & Winston.

Runco, M., et al. (1998). Personal Explicit Theories of Creativity. *Journal of Creative Behavior 32*(1), 1-17.

Scales, P. and Leffert, N. (2004). *Developmental Assets: A synthesis of scientific research on adolescent development*. Minneapolis, MN: Search Institute.

Siegel, D. (1999). *The Developing Mind: Toward a neurobiology of interpersonal experience*. New York, NY: Guilford.

Sizer, T. R., & Sizer, N. F. (1999). *The Students are Watching: Schools and the moral contract*. Boston, MA: Beacon Press.

Sorokin, P. A. (1954). *The Ways and Power of Love*. Chicago, IL: Henry Regnery Company.

Starkman, N., Scales, P. C., & Roberts, C. (1999). *Great Places to Learn: How asset-building schools help students succeed*. Minneapolis, MN: Search Institute.

Sternberg, R. J., & Barnes, M. L. (1988). *The Psychology of Love*. New Haven, CT: Yale University Press.

Symonds, P. M. (1946). *The Dynamics of Human Adjustment*. New York, NY: Appleton-Century-Crofts, Inc.

Tauber, R. T. (1998, December). Good or Bad, What Teachers Expect from Students They Generally Get! ERIC Digest. ERIC Document No. ED426985. Retrieved from http://eric.ed.gov/?id=ED426985.

Teacher Expectations & Student Achievement (2002). Downey, CA: Los Angeles County Office of Education.

Trout, J.D., (1999). *Why Empathy Matters: The Science and Psychology of Better Judgment.* New York, NY: Penguin Books.

Walsh, A. (1991). *The Science of Love: Understanding love and its effects on mind and body.* Buffalo, NY: Prometheus Books.

Weinhold. (2007). Available from The Carolina Institute for Conflict Resolution and Creative Leadership website: http://weinholds.org/

Werner, E. E., & Smith, R. S. (1992). *Overcoming the Odds: High risk children from birth to adulthood.* Ithaca, NY: Cornell University Press.

Wheatley, M. J. (1999). *Leadership and the New Science: Discovering order in a chaotic world.* San Francisco, CA: Berrett-Koehler Publishers.

Wheatley, M. J. (2002). *Turning to One Another: Simple conversations to restore hope to the future.* San Francisco, CA: Berrett-Koehler Publishers, Inc.

About the Author

Dr. Gerry Nolan has worked in both public and private educational settings since 1979. Throughout that time Gerry has served as a teacher, coach, principal, curriculum director, superintendent, and school board chair. Gerry and his wife, Lisa, have returned to northwest Montana, where they hope to never leave. They have three children: Katherine Marie, Mary Elizabeth, and Mackenzie James.

About Leonine Publishers

Leonine Publishers LLC makes fine Catholic literature available to Catholics throughout the English-speaking world. Leonine Publishers offers an innovative "hybrid" approach to book publication that helps authors as well as readers. Please visit our web site at www.leoninepublishers.com to learn more about us. Browse our online bookstore to find more solid Catholic titles to uplift, challenge, and inspire.

Our patron and namesake is Pope Leo XIII, a prudent, yet uncompromising pope during the stormy years at the close of the 19th century. Please join us as we ask his intercession for our family of readers and authors.

Do you have a book inside you? Visit our web site today. Leonine Publishers accepts manuscripts from Catholic authors like you. If your book is selected for publication, you will have an active part in the production process. This book is an example of our growing selection of literature for the busy Catholic reader of the 21st century.

www.leoninepublishers.com

www.ingramcontent.com/pod-product-compliance
Lightning Source LLC
LaVergne TN
LVHW011345080426

835511LV00005B/135